I WILL BUILD MY CHURCH

Biblical Insights
on
Distinguishing Doctrines
of the
Church of God

by
John W. V. Smith

Published by
Warner Press, Inc.
Anderson, Indiana

ISBN 0-87162-411-7
All Rights Reserved
Printed in the United States of America
Warner Press, Inc.
Arlo F. Newell, Editor in Chief

Contents

This book is dedicated
to those who translated
this document during
the Asian teaching mission venture
of 1981-82
by Dr. John W. V. Smith
from which this book sprang.

PREFACE

In this volume, published posthumously, Dr. John W. V. Smith completes a task for which he felt a special burden for a number of years. He wanted to provide the Church of God with a statement that would help it to address the problem of self-understanding and a sense of mission. This book is addressed to the layperson as well as to pastors, teachers, and church leaders.

Dr. Smith was admirably suited to perform such a service. He was an exceptionally well-trained scholar with a Doctor of Philosophy degree in Church history and Christian thought from the University of Southern California. He taught in this field and related subjects at Warner Pacific College, and from 1952 until his retirement he was professor of Church history at the School of Theology in Anderson, Indiana. From that time until his untimely death he, along with his wife, Margaret, served the church at large in conferences and special overseas missionary assignments. This present volume, in part, stems from his effort to communicate the heritage and teachings of the Church of God to Japanese, Korean, and Indian pastors and students.

The Quest for Holiness and Unity, published in 1980 as a part of the centennial celebration of the Church of God, was Dr. Smith's largest work, and it remains the best and most current history of this movement. Not only is it valuable for understanding this heritage, but it also identifies capably and lucidly the place where the Church of God fits into the stream of historic Christianity.

Other books written by Dr. Smith include *Heralds of a Brighter Day,* and *Truth Marches On.* His unpublished Ph.D. dissertation was titled "The Approach of the Church of God (Anderson, Indiana) and Comparable Groups to the Problem of Christian Unity."

To this may be added numerous contributions in the form of articles and Sunday School lessons. The mere listing of these written works is to recognize the tremendous influence that Dr. Smith has exerted in the church in helping to understand its heritage, its doctrine, and in understanding its mission. Beyond these written records belongs the many years of activity in the church and his influence on the life and thought of the students who studied with him. He was officially appointed the Historian of the Church in 1957. He did much to preserve for posterity the memorabilia of the church. This is housed in the archives located in the School of Theology. Too few among us saw as clearly as he the importance of both a sense of history and of destiny, and how to live out in daily life a truly ecumenical spirit.

This, his last volume, will serve the church well. Just a look at the chapter headings gives a clear indication of the scope of the book. Many will appreciate his decision to summarize the doctrines shared by Christian orthodoxy and with them his identification and clear explanation of those distinctive doctrines and emphases that help to identify the Church of God. True to his kindly and ecumenical spirit, this book is not polemical in nature. Rather it is a straightforward statement of the faith commonly shared in the Church of God. Those who use this book as a study guide will also appreciate the study questions prepared for each chapter.

Dr. Smith opposed, as did the early ministers of this movement, any effort to form creeds or to establish hard and fast statements of doctrine to be used as a test for fellowship. He did, however, know that every generation must put its faith in its own language and life even as it defends the "faith once delivered to the saints." This principle he expressed beautifully and practically in the last chapters on discipleship and the maturing Christian.

We shall miss John—his life, his mind, his gentle prodding, his skill of expression, his practical working out of his faith in the way he spent his life and his resources. For his friends it is hard to accept the fact that we now have in our hands the last book that John W. V. Smith will write. Of one thing we may be sure and in this we rejoice: He has "responded to the upward call of God."

Dr. Milo L. Chapman
Provost,
Warner Pacific College
Portland, Oregon
February 1985

INTRODUCTION

"What is the difference between the Church of God and any of the several hundred other groups of Christians, each carrying its own denominational label or name?" This question was asked by a young Japanese seminary student in Tokyo who was sincerely seeking for guidance regarding his own Christian ministry. In his land, only about one percent of the people acknowledge the lordship of Christ under any label. For him, the answer was very important. He was concerned about having the most advantageous setting for his Christian witness. He could not help but wonder if the opportunities might be greater in a larger group.

This young man is not alone in making such a query. All around the world this question is often asked both by persons who hear about the Church of God for the first time, as well as by those who have heard but know little about this particular religious movement. Strange as it may seem, this question is most often asked by persons within the movement itself. They are sometimes at a loss to precisely describe distinctive teachings or to differentiate this fellowship from other Christian groups. Many of the questions come because of the absence of any formal statement of faith to which they can refer. It is to this issue that this study is addressed. Its purpose is to identify and describe the essential character of the Church of God movement and to examine the biblical basis of its theological teachings and practices. A few preliminary statements are necessary to set the stage for such a study.

To begin with, a word needs to be said about the significance of theology in the Church of God. Throughout its whole history all that the movement has said and done has centered on doctrine. The fact that there has been no formulated creed does not in the least suggest an indifferent attitude toward theology. In fact, quite the opposite is true. The Church of God is a reform movement and the focus of that reform has been a return to solid biblical teachings without reference to creeds and sectarian distinctives written by councils and committees. Primary attention has been given to the message of the Word of God. The pioneer leaders spoke often of "the truth" and were vigorously zealous in sharing the "light" they had received from holy Scripture. It was doctrine that brought the movement into existence. It is only by continuing in sound biblical teaching that the Church

2

of God can fulfill its mission in the world.

Second, it must be noted that this study is not intended to be a textbook in systematic theology or a complete review of Christian doctrine. For instance, there are only brief and sometimes incidental references to such basic and important Christian themes as the doctrine of God, the doctrine of human personhood, the doctrine of the Person and work of Christ, and the doctrine of the Trinity. These and many other doctrines emphasized in the Church of God movement are basically in harmony with biblical truth as understood in the broad context of historic orthodox Christianity. Thus, there has seemed no need to deal with these generally held teachings in any distinctive "Church of God" manner. In no way should such omissions be construed to suggest that these doctrines are unimportant or incidental. Whatever is biblical and fundamental to the Christian faith has been emphasized in the Church of God.

Third, it is recognized that there is a cluster of doctrines, all of them biblical and all of them historically orthodox, which have been given particular emphasis in this religious movement. It is on these highlighted doctrines that this study will focus. In some instances the particularity of the emphasis is quantitative—because of the amount or the priority of attention which has been given to certain teachings. In other instances the distinguishing feature has been of a qualitative nature—because specific meanings and applications to certain doctrines have been considered biblically sound and appropriate for

3

making the Christian faith meaningful in today's world. Eight doctrines with some significant degree of particularity have been selected as "distinguishing" the theological stance of the Church of God.

Fourth, it is important to call attention to the fact that these eight doctrines to be dealt with are designated as "distinguishing"—not "distinctive." It is obvious that none of these is unique to the Church of God. Any one of these doctrines would be emphasized by many other Christian groups and some groups would interpret individual doctrines in exactly the same way as the Church of God. That is because all of them are thoroughly Christian and all are based on Scripture. This particular combination of teachings, however, each interpreted in the manner indicated, makes the Church of God approach distinctive and significant.

Finally, it should be noted that the Church of God has no "official" statement of doctrine except the Bible itself. Consequently, the choices in regard to which doctrines to label as "distinguishing" for the Church of God are those of the author and have not been so identified by any authoritative body. Moreover, the interpretations themselves bear no official stamp. They are those of a "native son" with long association with the movement. It is an attempt to faithfully articulate that which has been generally accepted and taught as biblical "truth." Even so, as with all theological writing in the Church of God, this is one person's voice. Some may differ at certain points. But that is part of the genius of the Church of God. In a group that takes a "whole Bible" stance in regard to its creed, foregoing the practice of issuing official interpretations, there must be considerable room left for flexibility in both emphasis and exegesis. It is thus possible to hold different opinions and still maintain good fellowship as brothers and sisters in the Lord.

Despite this stance of openness and flexibility, the experience of a century of "living with the Word" has sifted out those points that give identity and purpose to this movement. The movement, true to its early message, is still seeking to restore the holiness and unity of God's church in all its beauty and power. May the study of these chapters make the vision brighter, the mission clearer, and the witness wider and stronger.

"I have written you quite boldly on some points, as if to remind you of them again, because of the grace God gave me to be a minister of Christ Jesus to the [Church of God] with the priestly duty of proclaiming the gospel of God, so that the [Church of God] might become an offering acceptable to God, sanctified by the Holy Spirit."

—Romans 15:15, 16 (NIV)

Dr. John W. V. Smith
November 1984

5

Chapter 1

The Church of God Reform Movement—How it Began

Biblical Resources
Isaiah 48:17-20; 52:8-11
Ezekiel 20:34, 41.
Zechariah 14:6-7
2 Corinthians 6:14-18
Revelation 18:1-5

For Study and Discussion

1. What are the basic reasons why reformations have been needed in the Church?
2. What features do most religious reformations have in common? In what ways would you say the Church of God reform is different from others?
3. What were the particular circumstances that brought the Church of God movement into being?

4. Several of the scriptures used as a rationale for this movement were written in relation to the history of Israel. Can these be properly applied to the condition of the Church in the nineteenth century?

5. In withdrawing from the various denominations and launching a new movement, how did Warner and the other leaders answer the accusation that they were only starting a new sect and not demonstrating the Christian unity they talked about so much?

Suggested Group Activity

Ask each person in the group for a brief personal history of his or her relationship to the movement: How many years? How about parents, grandparents, or others? Where was contact first made and how? (There may be some interesting stories!)

Information and Issues

Why Reformations?

In the Old Testament there is the recurring story of God's chosen people, Israel, wandering away from their covenant relationship with Yahweh. Time and again prophets and other leaders called them back to the true worship of God. Likewise, in the almost two thousand years of its history the Church has experienced departures and deviations that have required calls to return to the true faith. Whenever truth has become enshrouded in error, whenever ritual has obscured spirit, whenever either people or systems have become corrupt, or whenever essentials have been replaced by incidentals—a God-inspired person or group has appeared on the scene seeking to restore the Church to its true character as the body of Christ and the people of God.

In general, it may be said that all of the "reformations" in the Church have aimed at one or more of four general objectives: (1) the correction of errors or distortions in teaching that had crept into the Church, (2) the removal of corrupt persons and practices, (3) the changing of unscriptural or outmoded systems and procedures that had developed, and/or (4) the reemphasizing of some aspects of the faith that had come to be either negated or neglected. These chapters will focus attention on a contemporary Christian reform movement that embraces all four of these objectives. It is known simply as the Church of God.

Church historians recognize that the general state of Christianity in the closing decades of the nineteenth century was far from ideal. Despite the appearance of revival movements in both Europe and America as well as the great surge of missionary activity by almost all Protestant denominations, there was extensive evidence that all was not well in organized Christendom. There were numerous "liberal" tendencies that brought the authority of Scripture into question and discounted the role of Jesus as divine Savior. Underneath an outward appearance of righteousness there was a pervasive laxity in upholding ethical and behavioral standards for both church members and ministers. The burgeoning denominational system had produced more than two hundred different "brands" of Christianity. Even though there were some significant efforts for Christian cooperation between these denominations, most were competing with each other and sometimes engaging in vicious efforts to overpower another. The time was ripe for major reform.

The Why and How of Reform

Into this "gilded age" context there appeared some spiritually sensitive and dedicated people. Understanding the nature of the situation, they proclaimed concepts and took bold actions that would revamp the whole structural pattern under which Christianity was functioning at that time. The focus of their concern centered on biblical teachings regarding the nature of God's church. Using the church of the New Testament as a model, they judged the churches of their day to be distorted in form, dimmed in vision, and deficient in standards. They were not content simply to suggest cosmetic changes; they went to the core of the problem, challenging the whole denominational system. They denounced the dividedness of the churches and the worldliness of humans deciding which persons would be accepted into the membership of a given church. They called all true followers of Christ to live a life of holiness and to abandon the "sinful sects" that separated them from each other.

These reformers found biblical support for this radical approach in the symbolic meanings derived from the many examples of God's warnings to Israel through the prophets about compromising with the pagan practices of Babylon. Isaiah, for instance, reports the word of the Lord to the people: "Leave Babylon, flee from the Babylonians! Announce this with shouts of joy and proclaim it. Send it out to the ends of the earth; say, 'The Lord has redeemed his servant Jacob' " (Isa. 48:20). He repeated the message later with even more vigor: "Depart, depart, go out from there! Touch no unclean thing! Come out from it and be pure, you who carry the vessels of the Lord" (Isa. 52:11).

The prophets made it clear that a clean break from all sinful cultures was a prerequisite for the restoration of the nation. Ezekiel voiced the divine promise: "I will bring you from the nations and gather you from the countries where you have been scattered—with a mighty hand and an outstretched arm and with outpoured wrath. . . . I will accept you as fragrant incense when I bring you out from the nations and gather you from the countries where you have been scattered, and I will show myself holy among you in the sight of the nations" (Ezek. 20:34, 41). The fulfillment of this promise of restoration would mark the end of the dark day of bondage and confusion. Zechariah spoke of this time as the "day of the Lord" and said, "On that day there will be no light, no cold or frost. It will be a unique day, without daytime or nighttime—a day known to the Lord. When evening comes, there will be light" (Zech. 14:6-7).

It should be noted that New Testament writers utilized these same warnings and promises, applying them to conditions in the first-century church. The Apostle Paul, for instance, cites these passages in order to stress the importance of making a complete break with the pagan culture of his day: "Do not be yoked together with unbelievers. For what do righteousness and wickedness have in common? Or what fellowship can light have with darkness? . . . 'Therefore come out from them and be separate, says the Lord. Touch no unclean thing, and I will receive you' " (2 Cor. 6:14, 17). The Apostle John uses the fall of Babylon as the symbol of God's ultimate triumph over the forces of evil as represented in the oppressive Roman Empire. Exultantly he anticipates its destruction: "Fallen! Fallen is Babylon the Great!" Then, after elaborating on her sins, he repeats the same warning that was given to Israel: "Then I heard another voice from heaven say: 'Come out of her, my people, so that you will not share in her sins, so that you will not receive any of her plagues; for her sins are piled up to heaven, and God has remembered her crimes' " (Rev. 18:1, 4-5).

The reformers in the late nineteenth century could also see some very relevant applications of such passages to the church in their own day. Babylon, the symbol of sin, compromise, and confusion, was an apt description of the distortions of the faith and the sectarian division that they saw around them. They believed God still had a holy people and that he was calling them out of all the sects in which they were scattered to return to "Zion"—the true church. The time was right for such a movement. It was the "evening time" when light had broken forth at the close of the dark day. Joyfully they sang:

> "Brighter days are sweetly dawning,
>   O the glory looms in sight!
> For the cloudy day is waning,
>   And the evening shall be light.
> Lo! the ransomed are returning,
>   Robed in shining crystal white,
> Leaping, shouting home to Zion,
>   Happy in the evening light."

Where and When

The Church of God reform movement had its beginnings in the midwestern region of the United States of America. The first apparent manifestations were in the states of Indiana, Michigan, Ohio, and Illinois. It is customary to speak of 1880 as the year in which it started. However, from available evidence it would be possible to designate 1877 or 1878 as times of special insights by some of the early leaders. The first overt action toward launching a movement, though, did not occur until October 1881 in a meeting near the village of Beaver Dam, Indiana.

Although this movement for the rebirth of the Church originated in America it soon spread to Europe, Asia, and Africa. Spiritually sensitive, devout, and courageous Christian men and women heard or read the message and responded with enthusiasm. Many said, "I hear you saying what I have believed for a long time, but I did not know that others felt this way also. Thank the Lord for the Truth!" Thus, it is not possible to identify a single person as a "founder" of the movement. There were several early leaders, however, who played a very significant role in the development of the work. Among these in America would be Daniel S. Warner, Joseph C. Fisher, A. J. Kilpatrick. To these must be added the names of A. D. Khan of India and Ukichi Yajima of Japan, who identified themselves with the message just a few years later. They and many more were captured by a vision of the rebirth of the New Testament concept of the Church. They were so caught up in a sense of significance for their message that they took great care to keep from calling attention to themselves as persons. They regarded the developing response to their activity as a work of God and not the product of their own leadership. They took advantage of every opportunity to tell their story.

Who Was This Man Warner?

Among the early leaders the name most often mentioned is D. S. Warner. A look at his record reveals that he hardly fits the image of a "reformer." Far from being a rebel or a wild-eyed fanatic, he had been a serious-minded Christian minister for fourteen years. Licensed by the General Eldership of the Churches of

God in North America (Winebrennerian), he had served as pastor of several congregations in Ohio. He also spent more than two years in home missionary work in Nebraska. Recognized as an evangelist, he had been successful in all of these ministerial pursuits.

Warner had grown up in rural Ohio. His parents were not church-going people, and it was not until he was almost twenty-three years old that he gave any serious thought to religion. One February night in 1865 he attended a revival meeting being held in a country schoolhouse. He responded to the call to come forward and dedicated his life to God. From that time he entered into a serious quest for spiritual truth. The first two years after his conversion were spent in attending college and in teaching public school. In 1867 he entered the ministry.

Warner never ceased to have an open mind about his beliefs and methods of work. In the early years of his ministry he was a strong opponent of the doctrine of holiness that was beginning to be emphasized by some Methodists and other church leaders at that time. In the year 1877, however, he became convinced that this teaching was supported by Scripture and that living a holy life was possible for those who had been sanctified by the Holy Spirit. He began to preach holiness with great vigor. Somewhat to his surprise other ministers in his denomination became quite critical of his new emphasis. This led to some difficulties and eventually resulted in the revocation, in January 1878, of his license to preach. After some time

he affiliated with the Northern Indiana Eldership of the Church of God. This small group
accepted holiness teaching. He became an active
leader, serving as an evangelist and editor of
their church paper. After three years, however,
he found that fellowship too narrow for his
expanding concept of truth. In October 1881 he
severed his connection with all sectarian structures. He declared himself to be in open fellowship with all true followers of Christ, unencum-
bered by any humanly made barriers.

A Movement is Born

If Warner felt very much alone at the time he
made his declaration it was not long until he
discovered that many others had been thinking
along such lines for as long, or longer, than he
had. Within the next few months a movement
began to take shape as other leaders and lay
persons from various churches added their witness. J. C. Fisher and his wife, Allie, from
Michigan, A. J. Kilpatrick in Ohio, and Jere-
miah Cole from Missouri were among the earliest ministers. Kilpatrick, a United Brethren pastor, had declared himself to be free from sectarian bondage even earlier than Warner. These
and many others showed themselves to be vigorous "flying messengers," proclaiming far and
wide this "truth about the church" that had
excited their own understanding.

Not Men But a Message

None of these early leaders in the Church of
God had any intention of launching a new

religious organization. That would only add to the division among Christians—the basic evil from which they were trying to escape. They were simply an unstructured group of people who were brought together by their common faith in Christ and their conviction that they had a message for the whole church. They had seen the "light" on the nature of the church. They were the possessors of the great realization that the will of God could never be fully accomplished until all true Christians were brought together in a common witness. They insisted that not only must persons redeemed by Christ live righteous lives, but they must also be in harmony and fellowship with one another. On the basis of these fundamental principles the Church of God reformation movement was launched into a world that desperately needed its vital and positive message.

Chapter 2

Historical Antecedents of the Church of God

Biblical Resources
Hosea 14:1-2
Matthew 16:18
Acts 2:41-47
Romans 12:1-2
2 Peter 2:1-3

For Study and Discussion

1. In what ways is the Israel of the Old Testament a prototype of the Church? What parallels can one see between God's repeated calls to Israel through the prophets to return to the way of righteousness and the call to the Church for reformation and renewal?

2. In what sense is it feasible to make the first-century church a model for the church of the present day?

3. Why would the reformations of the Church prior to the late nineteenth century be considered necessary and good but inadequate?

4. What particular religious conditions in America in the 1870s and 1880s made this area a particularly receptive field for reform?

5. Reformers always call attention to failures and shortcoming of the existing situation; they also must have some solutions to the problems they pose. What kinds of answers did the early Church of God leaders have for the questions they raised?

Suggested Group Activity

The descendants of many of the earlier reforming groups are still witnessing to the faith of their founders. Various persons may share their contact with or knowledge of such groups as the Franciscans, the Waldensians, Lutherans, Mennonites, Quakers, Brethren, Disciples of Christ, and various groups.

Information and Issues

How Old Is the Church of God?

The Church of God reform movement celebrated its centennial in 1980-81. But this was not a commemoration of the one-hundredth anniversary of God's church. Ever since his covenant with Abraham, God has had a "people" he calls his own. The Old Testament tells the story of God's dealings with this special people. He blessed them in their faithfulness, punished them in their wrongdoings, and called them to return when they wandered from his ways (Hos. 14:1-2). The New Testament tells the story of God's sending his Son Jesus to the earth as Savior and Lord, making it possible for humankind to have a new relationship with the divine. Thus, Jesus brought into being a new "people of God" which he called the Church (Matt. 16:18). So the Church of God, in its broadest sense, is as old as time. In the New Testament sense its beginning goes back to the time of Christ.

The Church has thus been in existence through twenty centuries. It now becomes important to review some highlights of this total history in order to understand the relevance of the reform movement that developed in the late nineteenth century.

The New Testament Church

Even though Jesus founded the Church he did not draw up any design for its structure. Apparently he left the impression that a special responsibility for the continuation of his work rested upon the Twelve. Thus, the remaining eleven rather quickly proceeded to select a successor to Judas (Acts 1:15-26). Something of the manner in which the early church functioned is described in Acts 2:41-47. The writer depicts an almost idyllic situation with the saints "praising God and enjoying the favor of all the people" (v. 47). The letters of Paul and other writings, however, indicate that the first-century church was not perfect and had to deal with many problems. Despite these imperfections the church described in the New Testament is the best model we have of the new "people of God." These are the ones Jesus delegated to carry on his work in the world (Acts 1:8). This story of the early development of the Church provides the basic foundation for the beliefs, structure, and mission for all time. In this fundamental sense it is the model for judging the faithfulness of the Church in any age or situation.

Deviations, Distortions, and Departures

Very early in Christian history, beginning even during the time the New Testament books were being written, there began to be additions to and departures from the New Testament pattern. This continued for several hundred years. These deviations are referred to as heresies and the process of "falling away" is called apostasy. For many centuries, Christian leaders were called upon to determine whether certain new teachings or practices were consistent with the basics of Christianity, or if they were actually leading in a direction that would destroy the faith.

The earliest teachers who put forth a threatening doctrine were those who projected the view that a person must first become a Jew in order to become a follower of Christ. Combating the Judaizers was the burden of several of the Apostle Paul's letters, especially Galatians. Then there were those who taught that the Christian message of freedom from the Jewish law gave one license to do anything. These first-century libertines were known as Nicolaitans

Country Living

Yes! I'd like to order COUNTRY LIVING!

☐ Please send me 10 issues for only $12.00
...that's a $13.00 savings from the single-copy price!

☐ I prefer 20 issues for only $24.00

☐ My payment is enclosed (or) ☐ Please bill me

_____
initial here

Name _____ (Please print)

Address _____

City/State/Zip _____

Country Living's single-copy price is **$2.50** a copy.
Canadian and foreign prices on request. Offer expires:
9/30/95. A Publication of The Hearst Corporation.
Your first copy will be on its way to you in 6 to 9 weeks.

Country Living 595
TBCL105

SAVE $13.00 from the single-copy cost

BUSINESS REPLY MAIL

FIRST CLASS MAIL   PERMIT NO 220   RED OAK IA

POSTAGE WILL BE PAID BY ADDRESSEE

Country Living

PO BOX 7136
RED OAK IA 51591-2136

(Rev. 2:6,15). In the second century a man by the name of Montanus was disturbed about the growing formality he saw in the church, a very valid concern. He claimed himself to be a personification of the Holy Spirit, the *paraclete* (John 14:16-17), who had come, as Jesus promised, to proclaim the truth. These are only a few examples of false teachings and teachers who appeared in the early centuries to threaten the Church.

Then, too, many Gentile converts to Christianity had been former devotees of various pagan philosophies such as Stoicism, Epicureanism, Platonism, and Gnosticism. Some aspects of these philosophies were compatible with Christianity, while other features distorted the faith. It was not always easy to separate the true from the false. Gnosticism especially made deep inroads into the Christian community, strongly supporting the concept of the deity of Christ but denying his humanity. The Apostle John's statement, "The Word became flesh and lived for a while among us," for example, is a strong anti-Gnostic affirmation (John 1:14).

In subsequent centuries many other doctrinal disputes arose. Many of these dealt with the nature of Christ and his relationship with the Father and the Holy Spirit. The most famous of these controversies dealt with the teachings of Arius, a presbyter in Alexandria, Egypt, in the late third and early fourth centuries. Arianism denied the equality of Christ the Son with God the Father. The debate became so intense that the unity of the Roman Empire was being threatened. Emperor Constantine called a general council of church officials to settle the matter. This council met at Nicea, in Asia Minor, in A.D. 313 and made Arian teachings a heresy. Their statement, known as the Nicene Creed, confirmed the doctrine of the Trinity, affirming the equality of the Son with the Father. It became the basic declaration of Christian orthodoxy for all time. Later councils dealt with related issues but none ever denied Nicea. This conciliar method of deciding what is Christian truth and issuing creedal statements became standard for the next several centuries.

Other problems arose in regard to the church's organization and structure. Since Christianity was new there were no established practices and Jesus gave practically no instruction along this line. Most early Christians were Jews; thus, it was only natural that many Jewish practices would be carried over and adapted to the new faith. The synagogue system, for example, became the model for the regular assembling of Christians for worship and study. The time was changed from the Sabbath to the first day of the week in commemoration of Christ's resurrection. Other procedures were borrowed or adapted from common practices in the culture of that day and from the political methodology of the Roman Empire. The development of the hierarchial structure of the Roman Catholic church is a good example of this kind of natural adaptation.

The result of all these developments was that by the time of the late Middle Ages the Church had become very institutionalized with strong central control. It was tightly creedalized, completely sacramentalized, predominantly clericalized, elaborately organized, and closely allied with the civil government. It became a state-supported institution during the late fourth century. By the sixteenth century there were many reasons why the Church was ripe for reform.

Reform Movements

Even before the great upheaval of the sixteenth century there were several significant attempts to get the Church back on the right track. By the fourth century there were many who felt the Church was becoming too much like the world, and so they withdrew from society and lived as hermits or monks in order to preserve their holiness. This practice was institutionalized in the monastic movement and came to be accepted by the Church. Later the medieval mystics, such as Francis of Assisi, claimed the privilege of direct access to God without having to go through a priest or participate in an approved ritual. In so doing they challenged both the clericalism and the sacramentalism that had developed in the Church. In the twelfth century several "anti-churchly" groups developed, mostly in southern France and northern Italy. They were known by such names as the Cathari (the Pure), Albigensians, and Waldensians. They emphasized personal salvation by faith and sought to live holy lives. The Albigensians were persecuted severely and finally annihilated. The Waldensians took refuge in the Italian Alps and survived, even to the present day. They are recognized as the first heralds of the Protestant reformation four-hundred years later.

The great era of religious reform came into full bloom in the sixteenth century when strong leaders such as Martin Luther, John Calvin, Ulrich Zwingli, John Knox, and others successfully challenged the powerful hierarchy of the Roman Catholic church by undermining the theological structure that supported it. They emphasized justification by faith rather than sacraments, the sole authority of the Bible rather than the pope, the priesthood of all believers rather than limiting the right of access to God only to ordained clergy, and the freedom of all Christians to regard their vocations as a calling from God rather than just the select few who took religious vows. Many historians speak of this reforming movement as a "religious revolution." Beginning in Germany and spreading to most other western European nations, it brought major changes to both the religious and political structures of the whole region.

There were other reformers in the sixteenth century, however, who felt that these major leaders did not go far enough. The Swiss Brethren and others advocated believers' baptism (rather than the baptism of infants), emphasized the necessity for holy living after conversion, and believed that the Church should be free and separate from the government. These people were called Anabaptists (re-baptizers). Eventually the various small groups were consolidated under the leadership of Dutch reformer **Menno Simons**, and they became known as **Mennonites**.

These far-reaching events of the sixteenth century did not end the need for reform, however. Since that time many more movements have developed with the avowed purpose of bringing the Church more in line with biblical teachings. It is important to mention a few of these. In seventeenth-century England, for instance, a group known as Puritans came into being. Their major concern was to purify the Church of England by removing some remaining Roman Catholic practices. They were persecuted by the established church and some were forced to leave England. Many of these displaced Puritans became the first settlers in the new world of North America. A group of radical Puritans under the leadership of George Fox were known as Quakers. They abolished both the ordained clergy and the sacraments altogether and set very strict standards for Christian behavior.

Another reform movement known as pietism developed in Germany during the eighteenth century and spread to England and other countries. The pietists sought to restore personal devotion for all Christians. They also encouraged Christian service and missions. This new emphasis on "heart and hand" religion resulted in the formation of new groups such as the Moravians and the Church of the Brethren. It also became a primary factor in generating the great evangelical wakening in England led by John and Charles Wesley, which means that pietism was a strong influence in the development of Methodism.

At various times in Christian history, and particularly since the sixteenth century, there have been times of renewed enthusiasm for deepening the commitment of believers. This was often accompanied by vigorous efforts to win new converts. These special times were appropriately called "revivals." Even though the primary thrust of such efforts has been renewal rather than reform, the impact of some has brought significant change in the character of the Church. The English evangelical awakening just mentioned would be a good example. The Great Awakening in America in the 1740s would be another, as would the Kentucky Revival on the American frontier around the year 1800. This latter movement initiated a particular approach to Christian experience that focused on the necessity of personal conversion. Being "born again" and receiving inner assurance of being "saved" came by accepting the redemption made possible through Christ's death on the cross. This approach came to be called "revivalism." Mass meetings were the chief method. Often they were held over an extended period of time. Sometimes they were conducted in open areas where people could set up temporary living accommodations and stay for several days. These were called camp meetings. Both the concepts and the methods of revivalism had a great influence on the development of Christianity in America and in many other parts of the world.

Two other movements need to be mentioned which have special significance as antecedents of the Church of God. The first of these developed on the American frontier in the wake of the Kentucky revival. In the early 1800s some leaders in that area, notably Thomas and Alexander Campbell and Barton W. Stone, became concerned about the growing number of divisions and sects in Christianity. They believed this was contrary to Christ's intention for the Church. Even though this effort toward Christian unity did not stem the tide of sect-making, it is a notable witness to the New Testament teaching that God has only one church and all true followers of Christ are members.

Another nineteenth century movement of special importance is the National Holiness Association, which was organized in 1867. Many Christian leaders had become concerned about the growing laxity in behavioral standards and what appeared to be an increasing worldliness in the churches. Focusing attention on biblical teachings in regard to holy living, they lifted up the doctrine of sanctification as the means for achieving this standard of Christian perfection. This came through the empowering work of the Holy Spirit. Following the language of John Wesley, they spoke of sanctification as being the experience of "perfect love" and as a "second work of grace" beyond justification.

The New Reformation

With this background—almost nineteen centuries of Christian history and many efforts for reform and renewal—the Church of God reform movement began. In many respects this reformation resembles several of the earlier reform movements. For example, there was strong preaching about justification by faith, the authority of the Bible, a "born-again" experience of salvation followed by the Holy Spirit's work of sanctification, and holiness in everyday living. There was also a major emphasis on what all of these teachings meant when related to God's one holy church. Thus, instead of limiting itself to one or two points of emphasis, such as previous reformations had done, this new movement sought to bring all biblical truth and all true Christians together in a unity of faith and fellowship. This would enable the Church to measure up the full extent of God's intention for it. From the standpoint of comprehensiveness other reformations had not approached the scope of vision and the ambitious hope of this one. The Church of God reformers "saw the church." They envisioned a bringing together of all faithful Christians into a visible unified fellowship that would transcend all divisions and surmount all sectarian walls.

Chapter 3

A Whole-Bible Basis
for Belief

Biblical Resources
Psalms 51; 58; 78:1-7; 117
John 14:21
2 Timothy 3:14-17

For Study and Discussion

1. Is it really possible for a group to be "distinctive" without separating itself from other similar-minded groups?

2. A Christian group formed in the nineteenth century, earlier than the Church of God, also rejected formal creeds and declared its position to be, "Where the Bible speaks, we speak; where the Bible is silent, we are silent." What is the difference between that view and the whole Bible approach of the Church of God pioneers?

3. It is obviously true that creeds do divide Christians from one another. Could it also be true that a statement of affirmation of commonly held beliefs could bind people together? Is there any difference between an "affirmation" and a "creed?" State reasons for your answers.

4. In what ways can creedal confessions become substitutes for a life-changing conversion experience?

5. The liturgical use of creedal confessions often becomes nothing more than "vain repetitions." Can affirmations of faith in worship enhance the meaning of such statements?

6. What responsibilities are placed on the interpreter when one takes a whole-Bible approach to the content of the Christian faith?

7. What are the problems of communicating and teaching the faith to children and new converts when the broad "whole Bible" is the standard?

Suggested Groups Activity

Develop, as a group, one or more strategies for using a whole-Bible approach to teaching faith to children, youth, and new converts in the church. How could this same thing be done in the home?

Information and Issues

The Big Problem and the Basic Remedy

In the "denominational" system, which has prevailed since the sixteenth century, each of the various separate Christian groups carries its own distinctive name and identifies its own particular practices and interpretations of the faith. Examples of these include Lutheran, Presbyterian and Roman Catholic. Points of difference usually are given special emphasis as a means of promoting group loyalty and enthusiasm. Each group describes itself as holding to the "truth" as opposed to the "notions" of others. The result is rivalry and sometimes bitter competition even though all groups claim to be faithful followers of Jesus Christ. In this context it is not surprising that almost any person associated with the Church of God has been asked, "What are the differences between your movement and other Christian groups?" or "What are the distinctive beliefs of the Church of God?"

Such questions are normal and they deserve an answer. But, for a group with a major concern for Christian unity the setting forth of a list of sharply defined distinctives poses a big problem. Identifying distinctives emphasizes differences and implies a claim to superiority; neither of these is consistent with the spirit of unity. Consequently, answering these questions about Christian beliefs and practices for which the Church of God movement would claim unique ownership is not simple or easy. There is sometimes a tendency for the responder to fall into the trap of naming a few items that would be different from most other Christian groups— such as having no formal membership ceremonies or roll books and observing the ordinance of foot washing—and thereby suggesting that these distinctives identify the Church of God. These, indeed, are true statements, but such a list, no matter how long, does not describe the character of the movement or state its purposes. A similar type of response is the attempt to delineate the movement in negative terms, such as nondenominational, nonpentecostal, non-Calvinistic, nonmillennial, and so on. Here again, the statements are true but the description is inadequate.

Still another response to the question about the distinctives of the Church of God is to answer in a more general way by saying that the movement is conservative in doctrine and evangelistic in method. Some would elaborate on this generalization by pointing out that this evangelical/revivalistic stance is rooted in an Arminian view of humankind that sees persons as free moral agents capable of accepting or rejecting the offered grace of God. These statements also are true, but they still fall short of identifying the movement since they do little more than describe some of its affinities with well-known theological positions and methodologies. Their effect is only to recognize that the movement is related to some historic Christian traditions and rejects others. To multiply such declarations of position moves in the direction of formation of a creed—and that the movement rejects. Certainly none of these approaches can adequately describe the Church of God.

How, then, can the distinctiveness of the movement be described without violating the concern for Christian unity, without appearing to be just another sect, and without affirming a set of propositions that would be interpreted as a creed? The answer lies in recalling the foundational theological principle on which the Church of God is based. An examination of the early preaching and writing reveals that one of the chief points of distinctiveness among the pioneers was their desire to preach all the truth of the gospel of Christ. It was this objective that brought the new reformation into focus in the minds of the early leaders. As early as 1878, D. S. Warner wrote in his diary, "The Lord . . . gave me a new commission to join holiness and all truth together and build up the apostolic church of the living God."

Because of this "all truth" ideal there was a deliberate attempt to embrace and emphasize all that was taught in Holy Scripture. They neglected none of the major doctrines of the Christian faith. They proclaimed the Bible as the Word of God and the only necessary rule of faith. They wanted nothing more than to be led by the Holy Spirit into an understanding of all the truth that God had for them. This comprehensive approach to "all truth" became the basis for all their teaching and preaching. Distinctiveness was not in particular points of emphasis but in the objective to emphasize all of God's truth as contained in his Word and revealed by his Spirit.

What Is Wrong with Creeds?

In declaring, "We have no written creed except the Bible; the Word of God is our only rule of faith!" the early leaders of the Church of God were making a very strong positive affirmation. Such a declaration also indicates a very negative position regarding the many brief statements of faith, known as creeds, that have been formulated by various individuals and groups through the whole course of Christian history. This would include such well known historic affirmations as the Apostles' Creed, the Nicene Creed, the Augsburg Confession (Lutheran), the Westminster Confession (Reformed and Presbyterian), the Thirty-Nine Articles (Anglican), and many others. The immediate and obvious question, of course, is, What could they possibly find wrong with all these carefully drawn historic statements describing the essence of the Christian faith? After all, most of these have been approved and officially adopted by some responsible body of Christians.

The objection to these creeds by early Church of God leaders was not that they disagreed so much with the specific content of these statements. In fact, with some flexibility in interpretation they would have been able to make most of the historic "I believe—" affirmations a part of their own testimony. What they objected to was the idea of using these humanly fashioned statements as complete formulations of Christian truth. An examination of the early literature of the movement reveals some of the reasons why they were opposed to creeds.

1. Creeds are "man made." Even though they might express truths found in the Bible and even use the language of biblical passages, they

are not the Bible. They are human interpretations—humanly selected, humanly devised, and humanly formulated. They may be beautifully phrased, but they are not the "inspired Word of God."

2. Creeds are inadequate and only partial statements of the Christian faith. They might correctly state or explain certain parts of biblical truth but they do not declare all of it. Only the whole Bible can embrace the whole of God's truth. Selective truth and partial truth are both inadequate and dangerous. To omit is to distort; to be selective is to elevate human judgment above "all of the words of this life" (Acts 5:20).

3. Creeds are divisive. Almost all creedal statements have been formulated to state the particular interpretations of the faith by a certain person, a party, a sect, or a denomination. They were originally intended to draw lines of distinction between that party or sect and all others. While they might serve to separate truth from error, in regard to certain aspects of the faith, the net effect of creeds has been to separate Christians from one another rather than draw them together.

4. In a practical sense, creeds tend to lessen the real meaning of the Christian faith. Since these brief, often beautifully worded, capsule statements of faith are used frequently in public worship as part of the ritual, the words become familiar and are often repeated without any thought of their meaning. The lofty affirmations tend to become mere formalities. Church of God pioneers objected to this "cold, dead formalism."

5. Creedal confessions tend to become a substitute for a "new birth" salvation experience. In many groups becoming a Christian requires only that one make a verbal confession of faith. This means that a person could repeat a creedal affirmation and be labeled a Christian without ever participating in a genuine life-changing experience of finding forgiveness through Jesus Christ.

These are valid objections; they are as true today as they were a hundred years ago. Only the whole Word of God can be an educated statement of our faith.

But What Do We Believe?

Having affirmed the principle of a whole-Bible basis of belief, one quickly realizes that the problem of being ready to give a brief account of one's faith is not solved. In fact, it becomes more complicated. The "whole Bible" is a big book—in reality a diverse collection of sixty-six separate books. There is no simple way to summarize its teachings. It is not organized with any systematic arrangement according to topics and themes. Much of it is historical with the teachings implied rather than stated specifically. Moreover, since the Bible was written many centuries ago in a cultural context very different from today, it is not always easy to apply biblical teachings to our own time and circumstance. How, then, can we know precisely what we believe? How can we describe and explain biblical truth in such a way that it can be shared and taught to others?

Translating the Bible is a tremendous task. Knowing the original languages is not enough. One must also know enough of the history of those ancient times to understand what was really happening, and have sufficient knowledge of the cultural settings to comprehend the full meaning of what was written. It would almost seem that biblical interpretation should be left to the professional scholars and theologians. Why not settle for allowing the experts to digest the contents of the Bible and provide us with a one-page summary? Certainly that would be simpler, but it would not be satisfactory, for we would be back to the point of the original objection made by the early Church of God leaders—a "man-made" creed. Their solution—and ours: "Back to the blessed old Bible!"

Principles for Biblical Study and Interpretation

While we may learn much from biblical scholars and theologians, the fact that we take the whole Bible as the basis of our own faith places the responsibility directly on each of us to be students of the Word. It would be well if we could learn biblical Hebrew and Greek and do translating for ourselves. But this is not feasible, and so we must lean heavily on the scholars. Beyond the translation there are a few basic principles for personal Bible study. These can help us to understand its teachings and guide us in applying them to our lives and in sharing them with others.

1. We must begin with a strong conviction that the Bible really is the only creed we need.

We accept as fact that the Bible is *our* "rule of faith" because it is the inspired Word of God to his people. This was the starting point for the early leaders of the Church of God. The 1981 General Assembly of the Church of God in America reaffirmed this principle by approving a resolution that stated: "This Assembly declares its convictions that the Bible truly is the divinely inspired and infallible Word of God. The Bible . . . is 'profitable for teaching, for reproof, for correction, for training in righteousness, that the man of God may be adequate, equipped for every good work,' (2 Timothy 3:16-17) and it therefore is fully trustworthy and authoritative as the infallible guide for understanding the Christian faith and the living of the Christian life."

2. We must recognize that all Scripture is to be interpreted under the direction and guidance of the Holy Spirit. It is important to remember that Jesus specifically designated the Holy Spirit as "the Spirit of Truth" (John 14:17). So we must study the Bible prayerfully and look to the Holy Spirit to open its meanings to us. This helps us guard against subjective private interpretations.

3. Each biblical passage must be studied in the context of its setting. True meanings can be understood only as we take into consideration the particular time and circumstances of each saying and story. For instance, Psalm 51 can be understood properly only after one knows that it was written by King David after he had been confronted by the prophet Nathan in regard to

his sins—committing adultery with Bathsheba and arranging for the death of her husband, Uriah. With this information David's anguished cry for forgiveness becomes very meaningful. Contextual study applies to every part of the Bible.

4. Biblical teaching must be understood in the light of the whole Bible rather than in selecting certain isolated texts in order to find support for a certain view or prove a particular point. For instance, some texts mention only God's wrath and judgment; other texts mention only his love and mercy. To understand the true nature of God as both judgmental and loving, one must utilize both kinds of texts. That requires a whole-Bible perspective.

5. One must be able to distinguish between the various literary forms used in the biblical writings. Many parts of the Bible are forthright and simply stated—narratives, commandments, promises, teachings, and so on. Other parts are written in figurative language, using symbols and imagery to convey the intended meanings. The historical books are mostly literal reports of events that happened. Some writings, such as the books of Daniel and Revelation, are largely made up of symbols that must be interpreted before the meaning can be understood. Jesus used both kinds of language. For example, John 3:16 is a literal forthright affirmation of God's redemptive plan; Matthew 6:25 ("Take no thought of what you wear") is figurative and does not mean one should go without clothes.

6. One must be able to distinguish between

those things that are permanently valid and those that are culturally dated. For example, references to the "four corners of the earth" (Isa. 11:12; Rev. 7:1) reflect the view of the world generally held at the time of these writings and are not to be cited as proof either that the world is square or that the Bible contains gross errors of fact about the universe.

7. It is important to give studied attention to sound biblical scholarship. This means a diligent study of Bible history, a careful examination of the words of the text (using the original languages, if possible), and becoming acquainted with the findings of the best biblical scholars. One must realize, however, that "scholars" also have biases and often select evidence to support a particular view and ignore a whole-Bible perspective. Thus, scholarship itself must be evaluated. Standard commentaries and a variety of translations may also help us become responsible interpreters of the Word.

8. Even though the Church of God has no formulated creed, it is important to be able to identify the essential aspects of the Christian faith. These essentials are not of our own making; they are the "truths" that are reiterated over and over again in the Word of God. Basically they deal with our understandings of God, of ourselves, and of the universe. They relate to the past, the present, and the future. All of these understandings must find their basis in the Bible and the meanings must be applied to our everyday life situations.

By utilizing these fundamental principles of biblical interpretation we shall be preparing ourselves to formulate our own theology on the basis of the whole Bible, which is our only creed.

Chapter 4

Basic Beliefs Held in Common with Other Christians

Biblical Resources
Romans 10:8-11
Philippians 2:5-11
Romans 3:21-24; 5:1-2
Galatians 2:15-16
1 Peter 2:4-5, 9
Revelation 1:5-6
Ephesians 4:1
1 Corinthians 10:31-33

For Study and Discussion

1. What values are there in noting ways we are like other Christian groups as well as ways we are different?

2. As you read the Nicene Creed, do you find specific points at which you would disagree? What essential aspects of the Christian faith are not mentioned? Do you understand what is meant by some of the unusual phrases, such as "very God of very God?"

3. Are Christians united by agreeing on a common affirmation of faith or by their testimony to a common experience of redemption through Christ? Can the affirming of a creedal statement be regarded as a testimony to having participated in a "born again" experience of salvation? Explain.

4. What do you understand to be the practical meaning of the Protestant Reformation teaching that affirmed the biblical doctrine of "the priesthood of all believers?"

5. What are the theological issues involved in the belief that church and state should be separated?

6. In addition to the doctrine of sanctification, what other beliefs or practices would the Church of God share with John Wesley and the eighteenth-century Evangelical Awakening?

Suggested Group Activity

Ask each person to take a few minutes to list specific concepts and beliefs that are important for Christians to experience. Combine these terms on the chalkboard. Assign a few terms to each person instructing them to write their own brief definition. (If you are working with a large group you might want to divide it into several smaller working groups, assigning each group several terms.) Make sure that all of the terms are assigned. After a few minutes, come together and share the definitions. This will provide for good discussion. Another idea is to have symbols drawn or constructed from chenille wire to represent each term. Be sure to have the creator explain what each symbol means.

Information and Issues

Different—But Alike

In calling attention, as this book does, to certain "distinguishing" biblical doctrines that have been and continue to be given special or particular emphasis in the Church of God movement, it must be clearly understood that the eight doctrines singled out for study do not stand alone. Behind them and along with them is the already mentioned whole body of biblical truth. Through nineteen centuries of Christian history before this movement came into being, many of these truths had been carefully studied. They had been refined through much discussion of variant opinions and, under the guidance of the Holy Spirit, had been accepted by devout followers of Christ as "orthodox" or correct and sound statements of doctrine. Consequently, there was no need to redefine or challenge those basic teachings that already had been adequately formulated. Such fundamentals as belief in a triune Godhead consisting of Father, Son, and Holy Spirit, belief in the divinity of Christ, and belief in the inspiration of Scripture were simply accepted and proclaimed without question.

Thus, the Church of God movement is not to be considered as some strange and off-beat Christian sect. There is nothing about its teachings that could be considered unorthodox or heretical. It is completely within the main stream of historic Christianity as far as basic Christian doctrine is concerned. Many recent scholars who have analyzed the movement have noted that the early leaders did not introduce a single "new" doctrine; all the theological insights they emphasized and preached had been articulated previously in the framework of orthodox Christianity. None of the great essentials of the historic faith were omitted and nothing of a foreign nature was added. The early leaders of the movement were reformers, but they did not twist or tamper with the basic tenets of the Christian faith. It is important to note some of the specific points at which they continued to carry on the "faith of the fathers."

I. Basic Doctrines Shared with Most Other Christians

Despite the many separated segments of Christianity and the wide variety of teachings that divide the multitude of denominations, sects, and movements, there is still a central core of beliefs that is accepted by almost all persons and groups who call themselves Christian. The obvious question, of course, is, How is one to know exactly what these commonly held beliefs are? Fortunately, there are some summary statements of the basic content of the Christian faith that were formulated quite early in the history of the Church, some of which have come to be extensively used throughout Christendom. Among several such statements the most widely accepted of these early formulations is known as the Nicene Creed. It is recognized and used in the Roman Catholic church, in all the Eastern Orthodox churches, and in many, if not most, of the Protestant churches. A look at this statement could provide a brief declaration of the basic beliefs of most Christians.

Such an exercise poses an immediate problem, however, for persons associated with the Church of God movement. As already noted, early leaders of the Church of God rejected all creeds and were very critical even of the idea of creating such statements of belief. Regarding the Bible as the only necessary declaration of faith, they refused to formulate a "man-made" creed for themselves and vigorously objected to using those that had been formulated by others. It must be recalled, though, that their objection was not because they disagreed with the content of these historic creedal statements; they took issue with the ways in which the creeds were used. Consequently, it would not violate the historic noncreedal stance of the Church of God to examine this most universally accepted affirmation of faith in order to identify the basic Christian beliefs held in common by most Christians.

To understand the nature of this statement and the purpose for its formulation, it is necessary to know something of its background. It is called the Nicene Creed because it was drawn up and approved by a council that met at Nicea, a town in northwest Asia in A.D. 325. This was the first ecumenical council (worldwide assembly) of Christian leaders. The council was called by the Roman Emperor Constantine for the purpose of settling a theological dispute that was raging throughout the Empire and causing considerable unrest. The issue was the nature of Christ: was he divine—the Son of God—or was he only an extraordinary man—a prophet of God? This latter position was the view of a faction led by Arius, a presbyter in the church at Alexandria, Egypt. He was opposed by the bishop in Alexandria and another strong leader from there by the name of Anthanasius. It was a very bitter debate. Eventually the council decided to reject the view of Arius and approved a statement declaring that Jesus was divine—of one substance with God the Father and equal with the Holy Spirit. The statement also summarized other commonly held Christian beliefs and included them in the document that was adopted. In 381 the Council of Constantinople reaffirmed a slightly expanded version of the statement and still later other minor changes were incorporated to become what is now known and widely used as the Nicene Creed. An examination of this ancient affirmation provides a good summary of the basic teachings that are held in common by almost all Christians. Translated from its original Greek, it reads:

We believe in one God,
the Father, the Almighty,
maker of heaven and earth,
of all that is, seen and unseen.

We believe in one Lord, Jesus Christ,
the only Son of God,
eternally begotten of the Father,
Light from Light,
true God from true God,
begotten, not made,
of one Being with the Father;
through him all things were made.
For us and for our salvation he came down
from heaven;
by the power of the Holy Spirit he became
incarnate
from the Virgin Mary
and was made man.
For our sake he was crucified under Pontius
Pilate;
he suffered death and was buried;
on the third day he rose again in accordance
with the Scriptures;
he ascended into heaven.
He is seated at the right hand of the Father,
he will come again in glory
to judge the living and the dead,
and his kingdom will have no end.

We believe in the Holy Spirit,
the Lord, the giver of life,
who proceeds from the Father;

with the Father and the Son

he is worshiped and glorified;
he has spoken through the Prophets.
We believe in one holy catholic and apostolic
Church.
We acknowledge one baptism for the forgive-
ness of sins.
We look for the resurrection of the dead,
and the life of the world to come. Amen.

A careful reading of this statement reveals
that the cardinal principles of the Christian
faith are set forth clearly and concisely. Even
though many Christians, including those in the
Church of God, might want to clarify or elaborate on some of the words or phrases (such as
"one baptism for the forgiveness of sins") the
affirmation stands as a basic declaration of the
essentials of the apostolic faith upon which
most Christians are agreed. Note particularly
the special emphasis on the divine lordship of
Jesus Christ and relate this to the strong Chris-
tological passages in Romans 10:8-11 and Philippians 2:5-11.

II. Beliefs Held in Common
with Mainline Protestants

In the sixteenth century the church in western
Europe experienced a great upheaval known as
the Protestant Reformation. Martin Luther,
Ulrich Zwingli, John Calvin, and other reformers challenged and rejected some of the teachings and practices that had developed in the
medieval Roman Catholic church. Out of these
reforms there emerged a new stream in Christian
history known as *Protestantism*—a word that

means "to testify in support of." Not all those who objected to the Roman Catholic church agreed with one another, however, and so different kinds of Protestants formed their own church structures and statements of faith. There came to be many groups but historians usually classify them under four main types. Three of these—the Lutheran, the Reformed and the Anglican—are generally referred to as "mainline" protestants.

The Church of God movement does not trace its roots directly to any of these types and, because of its commitment to New Testament Christianity, it has resisted even being called Protestant. Nevertheless, a number of the distinctly Protestant points of emphasis are so obviously biblical, and thus consistent with the stance of the Church of God. It therefore becomes important to identify beliefs held in common with the large body of Christians known as Protestants. Affinities with the mainline groups will be noted first.

A. Justification by faith. The proclamation of this biblical truth became the cardinal principle of the sixteenth century Reformation. Based on the clear affirmations in such passages as Romans 3:21-24 ("Righteousness from God comes through faith in Jesus Christ to all who believe") and Romans 5:1-2 ("Therefore, since we have been justified through faith, we have peace with God through our Lord Jesus Christ"), the reformers rejected the whole idea of earning salvation by good works. This meant discarding such merit-acquiring practices as pilgrimages, the veneration of relics, and the buying of indulgences. Luther's strong emphasis, after reading these passages, was that justification was by faith alone. Good works, including the sacraments, are admirable and expressive of the Christian life but they are not the means of salvation. Justification is a gift of God, received by faith in the atoning work of Jesus Christ.

B. The priesthood of all believers. During the Middle Ages it was taught that ordinary Christians could not approach God directly but must go through some ecclesiastically authorized intermediary such as a priest or a recognized saint. The reformers rejected this idea. Based on scriptures such as 1 Peter 2:5, 9 ("You . . . are being built into a spiritual house to be a holy priesthood") and Revelation 1:5-6 ("and has made us to be a kingdom and priests to serve his God and Father"), they affirmed that every believer has the privilege of approaching God. He or she can pray to God directly and receive answers directly from him. In the language of the New Testament this makes every believer a priest.

C. The sufficiency of the Bible as a basis for spiritual authority. Through the centuries the Roman Catholic church had developed the dogma that all authority in the Church was vested in the clergy and that supreme authority rested in the Bishop of Rome, commonly called the pope. This claim had come to be supported by church councils and was generally accepted in the Roman church. The reformers rejected this concept completely and affirmed that the

Bible was the basis of all authority in the Church. This Protestant challenge to the power of the papacy had the effect of making Scripture the sole foundation for both belief and practice. Thus the proclamation of the Word and the study of the Bible once again became central in the life of the Church.

D. The "divine calling" of every Christian. The medieval Catholic church taught that only certain persons, such as priests and those who took the vows of a religious order (monks and nuns), had a divine calling. Other vocations were regarded as secular and had no spiritual significance. The reformers, basing their views on such scriptures as Ephesians 4:1 ("I urge you to live a life worthy of the calling you have received") and 1 Corinthians 10:31 ("Whatever you do, do it all for the glory of God"), affirmed that every Christian is called of God to be a representative of Christ every day in and through any kind of honorable vocation in which he or she might be engaged. Thus Christian faith became an everyday affair and was not confined to certain prescribed religious rites and practices.

These are at least four of the biblical beliefs that the Church of God movement shares with mainline Protestants.

III. Beliefs Held in Common with "Radical" Protestants.

In the sixteenth century there were many sincere people who felt that the major reformers did not go far enough in their rejection of

Roman Catholic beliefs and practices. Many "radical" groups, such as the Swiss Brethren and the Hutterites, sprang up in central and western Europe. Most were generally referred to as Anabaptists. In the 1540s several of these independent groups were consolidated under the leadership of Dutch theologian Menno Simons, and so they came to be called Mennonites. In later centuries the Quakers, the Pietists, some of the Puritans, and others were added to the list of radical Protestants. A review of the major beliefs of these groups reveals some very significant points at which biblical truth is commonly held with the Church of God.

A. Believers' baptism. Unlike the major reformers these groups rejected the practice of infant baptism. They contended that baptism should be according to the words of Christ: "He that believeth and is baptized shall be saved" (Mark 16:16, KJV). Thus, belief must precede baptism, and infants were incapable of that. They advocated that all adult believers should be baptized even though they had been baptized as infants; hence they were called Anabaptists (re-baptizers). This brought great persecution on them from both Catholics and Protestants who regarded this as blasphemy.

B. The restoration of the New Testament church. The radicals believed that the New Testament provided the model for what the Church in all ages ought to be. Above all, they taught that the Church should be a holy community composed of people who are separated from the world (2 Cor. 6:16; James 1:27; 1 John 2:17-17).

To insure a pure church they established strict rules for personal conduct and enforced them through discipline by the community as set forth in Matthew 18:15-17. Some of the groups, such as the Hutterites, took literally the Jerusalem arrangement described in Acts 2:42-47 and held all their property in common. (This group, incidentally, is still in existence with several communities in the north central United States and western Canada.)

C. Separation of church and state. The major reformers were content to continue the medieval system of having an "established" church—one that had the exclusive approval of the state and was supported by the government through tax funds. The radicals considered the Church a divine institution and believed that it should be completely separated from civil and secular authority and support. This principle later became the foundation for the concept of religious liberty.

D. The Christian conscience abhors participation in war. The radicals were strong believers that, since Christ was the Prince of Peace, his followers should not engage in activities that would result in death or injury to other persons. This view resulted in severe persecution by governments that compelled all able-bodied young men to serve in the military. In recent times some governments of the world recognize "conscientious objectors" to participation in war and allow youth to substitute some kind of nonmilitary service. Even though the Church of God is not one of the historic "peace" churches (such as Mennonites, Quakers, and Brethren), many young men in the Church of God are conscientious objectors to war and take advantage of the opportunity for alternative service in countries where this is possible.

IV. Beliefs Held in Common with Other "Holiness" Groups.

A number of separate Christian groups that have many things in common are brought into a special affinity with each other in that they give specific emphasis to the New Testament doctrine of sanctification. This is seen as a distinct work of God's grace for the believer. Along with such denominations as the Free Methodist, the Wesleyan church, the Church of the Nazarene, the Salvation Army, and others, the Church of God follows the interpretation of Scripture set forth by John Wesley. In the eighteenth century he affirmed that a holy and sinless life is possible for believers who consciously receive the Holy Spirit as their sanctifier, enabler, and guide. Since all of these groups were strongly influenced by the holiness movement they are thus brought into a close theological relationship with each other, upholding a similar interpretation of the biblical teaching on sanctification.

It becomes apparent, then, that the Church of God movement owes a great debt to many earlier seekers after biblical truth and in reality holds much in common with a wide variety of other Christians. To recognize this commonality is to pay tribute to many faithful, diligent, and serious scholars, church leaders, and reformers who have gone before. It must also be recognized, however, that there are a number of particular important biblical teachings to which this movement has given special emphasis. These will be noted and expounded in the next eight chapters.

Chapter 5

Salvation

Biblical Resources
Psalm 51:5
Matthew 1:21; 9:16-17; 20:28
Romans 3:23; 7:19; 10:9-19
2 Corinthians 5:12
Ephesians 1:7; 3:14-19
1 Thessalonians 5:23

For Study and Discussion

1. Almost all of the world's religions offer some procedure for "salvation." Why is this human need so universally recognized?

2. What is distinctive about the Christian "plan of salvation?" Define the words *grace* and *faith* as related to the Christian concept of salvation.

3. The common use of the word *saved* denotes that one would be rescued from some danger, such as saved from drowning or from a

burning building. What is a person saved from when he or she experiences salvation in a Christian sense?

4. In song, sermon, and testimony one hears a great deal about the joys of salvation. Make a list of the benefits of being "saved."

5. All Christians do not agree regarding the procedure for obtaining salvation through Jesus Christ. What are the differences between the sacramental, the confessional, and experiential views of the way to salvation?

6. Full salvation, according to the general understanding of Scripture among Church of God theologians, includes both justification and sanctification. Define these two terms and explain why it is important to designate both in describing salvation.

7. List what you consider to be the three most important aspects of the Spirit-filled life.

Suggested Group Activity

Each person should take a few minutes to list the benefits of being saved. Come together and share these lists, combining them into one list on a chalkboard. Next, you may ask each person to write a prayer of thanksgiving for God's goodness. Another activity is to have each person write a testimony according to the following formula. This is for a three-minute testimony about becoming a Christian.

1 minute: What it was like before I was a Christian.

½ minute: How I felt the call of Christ and responded.

1½ minutes: What life has been like since I became a Christian, identifying several benefits.

Suggest that each person be quite specific but not to the point of bragging, embarrassment, or vulgarity. It may be advisable to allow persons to work on this assignment at home during the week and bring their testimony in for sharing in the next session.

Information and Issues

The doctrine of salvation for all humankind through the death of Christ on the cross is the central theme of the Christian gospel. As the already-cited Nicene Creed states: "For us and for our salvation he came down from heaven." A plan of salvation, however, is not the sole property of Christianity. Most religions of the world offer some kind of "salvation" to their adherents. It is important, then, to understand the real nature of what seems to be a universal human problem and to explore the basic content of the various approaches to solving it.

Why Is Salvation Needed?

All people, regardless of race, tribe, color, nationality, sex, or station in life, have problems. Each person or group is seeking for solutions to the particular problems that plague their lives. The various religious systems find acceptance because they set forth certain procedures that are supposed to provide the needed solutions. In most of the eastern religions (Hinduism, Buddhism, Taoism, Jainism, and others) the solutions are related to their concepts about the causes of suffering and evil. In most religious systems suffering is regarded as being caused by supernatural forces in the universe, both good and evil, which often are personified as gods, goddesses, spirits, or demons. Salvation comes, then, by following certain prescribed acts or ceremonies designed to please these forces or to counteract their evil influence. In some religions suffering is thought to be caused by ignorance of how the universe operates. Salvation is thus to be found in using some secret key to understanding—a key that has been discovered by or revealed to the founder or some prophet of that religion. Still other religious systems believe that suffering is caused by human desire. Salvation is to be found in conquering that desire by self-denial, asceticism, and deliberate rejection of anything that might bring pleasure. Some religions see suffering as inevitable, and so they offer only the hope that by following certain practices the pain can at least be reduced in some future existence or state of being beyond this life.

Christianity also is concerned about human suffering but it has no simple answer regarding the cause. Some suffering is regarded as being caused by ignorance, some by carelessness, and some is recognized as being unexplainable. Suffering itself, however, is not considered to be humanity's real problem. In Judeo-Christian thought the basic problem of all humankind is sin, which is also a cause of suffering. The psalmist testified for all people when he wrote, "Behold, I was brought forth in iniquity, and in sin did my mother conceive me" (Ps. 51:5, RSV). The Apostle Paul reaffirmed this universal problem by declaring, "For all have sinned and fall short of the glory of God" (Rom. 3:23, RSV). Thus sin is rooted in the very nature of the human species. God created male and female "in his own image" (Gen. 1:27, RSV), which included freedom of choice between right and wrong. The Genesis story tells how the first pair of human beings chose to disobey God's command, and the human inclination ever since has been to follow their example.

In the Bible sin is described in two ways. The first is this universal tendency to make the easy wrong choices rather that the hard right ones. It is referred to as "missing the mark" or "falling short." The Apostle Paul's testimony regarding his own problem in Romans 7:14-24 is a good example of this definition of sin. The second usage of the word defines sin as rebellion against God or acts of transgression against God's law. The Apostle John refers to sin in this sense as "lawlessness" (1 John 3:4). Transgressions may be in the form of wrongful acts (either doing bad things or not doing good things) or they may be in the form of evil attitudes and feelings, such as prejudice, hatred, lust, or jealousy. Any of these sinful deeds or feelings may result in physical suffering and, for the conscientious person, will also result in mental suffering because of feelings of guilt and remorse. Even in cultures that have no clearly defined concept of sin or guilt there is still recognition of the same condition by reference to "bringing shame" or "losing face." These are caused by failure to live up to expectations or disobedience to the ethical codes of that culture. Sin, by any name, is a terrible burden to bear. Ultimately, in the Christian view, it leads to death and eternal separation from God. Human beings thus desperately need some means to overcome sin and escape its consequences.

"What must I do to be saved?"

The above question was frantically asked by the man in charge of the jail at Philippi where Paul and Silas were being held for preaching about Christ and were miraculously freed by an earthquake (Acts 16:30). It voices the deep concern of all humanity. The "gospel of Christ" is really nothing more than the good news that God has provided a wonderful and adequate answer to this question. This was the announced mission of Jesus in the world: "Thou shalt call his name Jesus; for he shall save his people from their sins" (Matt. 1:21, KJV). This is a declaration of God's purpose to conquer the power of sin and to elevate his people to a life of victory over sin. This plan of God for the salvation of all people through sending Jesus into the world is confirmed by many prophesies in the Old Testament and is declared in the whole of the New Testament. Salvation—deliverance from sin and its consequences—is now possible and available to every person.

All Christians rejoice in the promise and fulfillment of salvation through God's gift of Jesus but all do not agree on the procedure for receiving this gift. The answer given by Paul and Silas to the Philippian jailer's question suggests a relatively simple formula: "Believe in the Lord Jesus, and you will be saved—you and your household" (Acts 16:31). The meaning of the phrase "believe in the Lord Jesus" leaves room for various interpretations, however. The various views generally fall into one of three categories.

1. The confessional view. Those who hold this viewpoint give primary emphasis to the words *believe* and *confess* which appear in several scriptural passages relating to the manner of salvation. (In addition to Acts 16:31 note also Acts 8:37; Romans 10:9; 1 John 4:15.) Salvation becomes a reality, it is contended, when one affirms his or her sincere belief in the saving work of Christ. Thus creedal statements authorized by each particular group become very important, for they formulate the wording of the belief that one must affirm and accept in order to receive salvation.

2. The sacramental view. Many Christian groups relate salvation to the performance of the sacrament of baptism in the name of Christ. They cite the fact that in many New Testament passages baptism is associated with incidents of salvation. At the event in Philippi just cited, for example, it is reported that "immediately he [the jailer] and all his family were baptized" (Acts 16:33). Earlier, in Peter's sermon at Pentecost he exhorted his hearers, "Repent and be baptized, every one of you, in the name of Jesus Christ so that your sins may be forgiven" (Acts

2:38). The Apostle Paul, in his testimony at Jerusalem concerning his own salvation, reports that he was told by Ananias, "Get up, be baptized and wash your sins away, calling on his name" (Acts 22:16). These and other passages lead several groups to hold that Christian baptism is an act that in itself results in salvation. To assure the salvation of children they, accordingly, should be baptized soon after birth, say the proponents of this view.

3. The experiential view. Many other Christians give primary attention to the "new creation" emphasis regarding salvation that appears prominently in the teachings of Jesus and elsewhere in the New Testament. The key reference is the reply of Jesus to the query of Nicodemus: "I tell you the truth, unless a man is born again, he cannot see the kingdom of God. . . . You must be born again" (John 3:3, 7). The imagery is strengthened as Jesus adds the metaphors of "new wine" (Matt. 9:17) and "new garments" (Luke 5:36). Paul also speaks forcefully regarding an experienced change: "Therefore, if anyone is in Christ he is a new creation; the old has gone; the new has come!" (2 Cor. 5:17). This emphasis obviously gives sharper focus to the personal experiential aspects of salvation: decision, repentance, restitution, conversion, forgiveness, and assurance. "Confessing Christ" and "baptism" are not negated but become the outward witness to an inner divine work of re-creation that already has taken place. Those who emphasize this view generally are referred to as evangelicals. The Church of God would fit into this category.

What Does It Mean to Be "Saved?"

There are several words that are used in the New Testament to describe what really happens when one experiences salvation through Jesus Christ. The "new birth" (regeneration) and "conversion" (turning around) are but two of these. Perhaps the most commonly used descriptive term, however, is *justification*. (Note Romans 3:24; 4:25; 5:9). This word, which in a theological sense means "being made acceptable to God," carries almost the whole import of the Christian faith. It conveys the message that God has offered humankind a way to solve the problem of sin. That way is not the way of struggle and defeat or trying to counterbalance bad deeds with good ones; it is the way of forgiveness—blotting out the past record and starting anew. Such inclusive forgiveness could not come casually or cheaply. Sin is awful and its magnitude is universal. Justification could come only out of a great love and a willingness on God's part to demonstrate that love in a dramatic and costly way—to send his only Son to earth to be born and live as a human being, to die an unjust death, and then to conquer death by resurrection and return to the Father. The significance of this historical event is summarized in two words: *incarnation* (God became flesh) and *atonement* (satisfactory reparation or remedy for sin). Salvation, then is the love of God the Father and the work of God the Son combined to make forgiveness and justification possible for all repentant sinners.

Another word with a similar meaning and the

same implication is *redemption,* which means "to rescue, or to repurchase." The writer of Ephesians describes it well: "In him we have redemption through his blood, the forgiveness of sins, in accordance with the riches of God's grace that he lavished on us with all wisdom and understanding" (Eph. 1:7-8). Still another term frequently used in Scripture to describe salvation is *reconcilation,* which means "to bring back to harmony." Immediately following his reference to salvation resulting in a "new creation," the Apostle Paul enlarges on his intended meaning. "All this is from God, who reconciled us to himself through Christ and gave us the ministry of reconcilation: that God was reconciling the world to himself in Christ, not counting men's sins against them. And he has committed to us the message of reconcilation" (2 Cor. 5:18-19). Justification thus brings sinful human beings into harmony with God.

It is wonderfully important also to give special emphasis to a point already mentioned: this justification is freely available to every person in the whole world. Anyone who is willing to repent of his or her sins and forsake them can be saved. The only requirement is faith—belief and acceptance of the fact that the sacrificial death of Jesus really does offer forgiveness for sin and deliverance from guilt. One is then ready to receive this freely offered gift of God— to accept Christ as Savior. When this happens one knows that a change has taken place. It is an identifiable event. It is perfectly proper to speak of an "experience" of salvation. A person is a "new creation." Being released from the burden of guilt and shame, that person has become a candidate for the call to holiness.

Is There More?

These basic aspects of experiential salvation are proclaimed by most evangelical Christian groups around the world. There is another aspect of salvation, however, which is not so widely emphasized in a specific way. This is referred to as "sanctification" and has been given special attention mostly by a cluster of Christian groups commonly called "holiness" churches. In general it may be said that these groups follow the biblical insights on this subject expounded by John Wesley, a great leader of the evangelical awakening in eighteenth century England. A century later in both England and America there was a revival of interest in this Wesleyan teaching and there emerged what came to be called the "holiness movement." The reformers who became the early leaders in the Church of God movement were captivated by this teaching and made it their own because they were convinced that it was biblical truth. Sanctification has been a point of strong emphasis throughout the history of the Church of God.

Sanctification is understood to be a continuation of or a second stage in the salvation process, a "second work of grace" leading to "full salvation." It is not that justification is a partial or inadequate re-creation; it truly brings total forgiveness for past sins and restores one to complete harmony with God. But even in the midst of the joy of being forgiven there is an awareness that one is still human—that there remains an inclination to repeat those same sinful acts. It is then important to remember that even as it is impossible for a person to be justified except through the supernatural work of God through Christ, so also it is not possible for one to have continued victory over sin without supernatural assistance. The New Testament clearly teaches that this kind of help is available. *Sanctification* (or *sanctify*) is the word used to describe it.

The Apostle Paul is helpful in identifying both the problem and the remedy. In the midst of a discourse to the believers at Thessalonica, exhorting them to refrain from several specific sins, he burst in with the good news about how they could do this: "For this is the will of God, your sanctification. . . . For God has not called us for uncleanness, but in holiness" (1 Thess. 4:3, 7, RSV). In concluding this letter Paul reaffirmed and further described the help available for victory over sin: "May God himself, the God of peace, sanctify you through and through. May your whole spirit, soul and body be kept blameless at the coming of our Lord Jesus Christ. The one who calls you is faithful and he will do it" (1 Thess. 5:23-24). Sanctification, then, is a state of being "kept blameless," of being "made holy," or being "set apart for holy purposes." Most New Testament texts relating to sanctification either state or imply that it is a completed event or a continuing experience.

Among those who give emphasis to the doctrine of sanctification there has been general agreement that this work of grace is fashioned and given by the Holy Spirit. There is good reason for this. Several scriptural texts make this specific assertion. For example, Paul, in making reference to the Gentiles, refers to them as being "sanctified by the Holy Spirit" (Rom. 15:16). First Peter 1:2 uses the phrase "sanctifying work of the Spirit." In 2 Thessalonians 2:13 Paul notes that "God chose you to be saved through the sanctifying work of the Spirit and through belief in the truth." Even more significant is the promise of Jesus that he would send "another advocate" or "counselor" who is identified as "the Spirit of truth," to be with us forever. He is the "Holy Spirit," declared Jesus, "whom the Father will send in my name" (John 14:16-17, 26, RSV). Certainly this fits well the role of helper and sanctifier. Then, too, the phenomenal experiences of the believers at Pentecost, and on other occasions when the Holy Spirit "fell" on them, resulted in victory over their limitations and empowerment. Such would strongly support the view that sanctification is accomplished through the work of the Holy Spirit.

It cannot be ignored, however, that other texts are not so limiting in identifying the sanctifier. In Jesus' prayer he petitions the Father to "sanctify them [his followers] by the truth" (John 17:17). Paul's benediction on the Thessalonians, already noted, refers to "God himself" as the sanctifier. At other points Paul refers to "those sanctified in Christ Jesus" (1 Cor. 1:2). Likewise, in Paul's report of the voice of Christ which he heard on the road to Damascus he quotes Jesus as saying "Those who are sanctified by faith in me" (Acts 26:18). Another text suggests that the believer may contribute to his own sanctification. In writing to Timothy, Paul says, "If a man therefore purge himself . . . he shall be a vessel unto honor, sanctified, and meet for the master's use" (2 Tim. 2:21, KJV).

This variant phraseology really poses no problem. The New Testament writers had not precisely developed the concept of the Trinity, and so they made no distinction between the members of the Godhead. All texts agree that sanctification is a divine work in the heart of believers, giving them power to overcome temptation and enabling them to live a life free from any intentional transgression of God's will or way.

Chapter 6

Holiness

Biblical Resources

Matthew 5:2-11, 48; 16:24
Romans 6:12, 22; 12:2
1 Corinthians 1:2
Galatians 5:22-24
Colossians 1:28
Titus 2:11-14

For Study and Discussion

1. How can one account for the fact that all religions that relate their faith in any way to human behavior also express some form of aspiration to holiness?

2. What is the reasoning behind the widely held concept that asceticism (self-denial) produces holiness?

3. Explain the relationship between holiness and wholeness. Can a person have one without the other?

4. Can a distinction be made between inner holiness and outer holiness? How are the two related?

5. Explain the implications of the words used by the Apostle Paul in his salutation to those very imperfect people in the Corinthian church, referring to them as being "called to be saints" (1 Cor. 1:2, KJV).

6. How can one interpret that seemingly impossible admonition of Jesus: "You . . . must be perfect, as your heavenly Father is perfect" (Matt. 5:48, RSV)?

7. Jesus made it plain that he expected his followers to be witnesses to him. Someone has said, "We witness to Christ more by our ways than by our words." Evaluate this statement.

Suggested Group Activity

Encourage each person to list something that prevents him or her from being "perfect" like the heavenly Father. Do not sign these. Fold them and place them in a bowl or hat. Pass the bowl around, having each person draw out one to pray about during the coming week.

Information and Issues

It has been noted that evangelical Christians give strong emphasis to the importance of a personal conversion experience, or being "born again." Some (including the Church of God) go a step further and uphold the need to "go to perfection," or to be sanctified through a second work of grace. This is the only way to participate in the full salvation that God offers to all persons. In each case the primary focus is the significance of these one or two spiritual "experiences"—being "saved" and being "sanctified." It also is important, however, to recognize that these experiences, which often are climactic and clearly identifiable as to time and place, are not just events to be remembered as past moments of exhilaration. They mark a new ordering of one's total life-style. Forever after one's behavior and actions, as well as beliefs, attitudes, values, and aspirations are focused in a new direction— that direction being toward the "way of holiness" (Isa. 35:8, KJV). What are the involvements of this new way of life?

Aspiration to Holiness

Despite all the sin and evil in the world there is no culture on the earth that does not encourage some demonstration of holiness. On a very crowded street in the city of Benares, India, for example, a bearded barefoot man in dirty, tattered clothing was waving his arms and wildly shouting protests as a tourist aimed a camera at him. A tour guide quickly explained: "That is a holy man and he objects to being photographed. Please respect him." As the man moved on the guide observed that this "holy" man, along with hundreds of others in this city considered sacred by Hindus, had no family, no home of his own, and usually slept on the streets. He begged for all of his food and spent his days wandering about or in the multitude of shrines and temples in the city and along the hallowed Ganges River. This man serves as a reminder that, not only in Hinduism but in all of the world's major religions, there is a desire to achieve holiness. In most cases, however, this aspiration is expressed by only a selected few persons. Certain persons either choose, or are chosen to be called "holy." They may be called monks, nuns, shaman, lama, priests, or any of several other designations. They usually wear some distinctive garb or other symbol to indicate to other people that they are holy persons.

In all religious systems except Christianity the primary mark of holiness is asceticism. Self-denial seems to be universally regarded as both the way to achieve holiness and the outward evidence of it. Most persons designated as holy deny themselves. Many commit themselves to a life of chastity. They sometimes live in isolation from society as hermits. They allow themselves only the simplest of food and may engage in fasts and go without food altogether for long periods of time. They live in the humblest kind of quarters; often they have no shelter at all. Usually they have no personal possessions except their clothing; the usual means of livelihood is begging. In these and other ways they deny themselves in order to achieve holiness. Self-imposed suffering is regarded as purifying.

The Christian Expectation

There is a strain of asceticism in Christianity also. Jesus said, "If anyone would come after me, he must deny himself and take up his cross and follow (Matt. 16:24). He also spoke of the blessedness of being persecuted "for righteousness' sake" (Matt. 5:10-12). Likewise, on several occasions the Apostle Paul makes a special point of his own sufferings for the cause of Christ. In the early Christian centuries persecution and martyrdom came to be regarded as qualifying one for sainthood. During the Middle Ages, asceticism came to be widely practiced in the Roman Catholic church and was institutionalized in a system called monasticism. "Orders" of "religious" (holy) men and women were established. Vows of poverty, chastity, and obedience enabled these people to live separated from the sinful world. They dressed in a distinctive way and devoted their time to prayer, contemplation, and Christian service. The Protestant reformers of the sixteenth century rejected the whole system of monasticism, however, because it implied that only a select few Christians needed really to be holy; the rest could be much less holy and still please God. The monastic system also implied that it was necessary to withdraw from society in order to be a holy person. The reformers did not accept these ideas. Remembering that Jesus had said, "I have come that they may have life, and have it to the full" (John 10:10), they believed that every Christian could and should live as a godly and righteous person in the normal activities of family life, work, and leisure.

It is important to note that this view was not a rejection of Jesus' admonition regarding self-denial; rather it was a rejection of the idea that one can become holy by self-effort. It was an extension of the concept of salvation by faith and not works. Self-denial is a characteristic of the Christian life, but asceticism is not the way to holiness.

Perfection in Christ

In the Church of God movement there has been basic agreement with the Protestant view on these matters. However, there are some specific points of biblical interpretation in this movement that lead to a stronger emphasis and a sharper focus on the doctrine and practice of holy living than is true in most other church groups, except those few that designate themselves as "holiness" churches. This results in differences that need to be noted and their significance explained.

To begin with, there is a recognition of, and a willingness to take seriously, and literally, the many New Testament admonitions to holy living. Even the very imperfect people in the Corinthian church, for instance, were referred to by the Apostle Paul as "those sanctified in Christ Jesus, called to be saints" (1 Cor. 1:2, RSV). In the Colossian letter Paul also speaks of every man being "perfect in Christ" (Col. 1:28, KJV). James speaks of being "perfect and complete, lacking in nothing" (James 1:4, RSV). The writer of Hebrews not only admonishes but issues a warning: "Make every effort to live in peace with all men and to be holy; without holiness no one will see the Lord" (Heb. 12:14). The New Testament abounds in many more references urging holiness, sanctification, saintliness, newness of life, righteousness, and godliness. The capstone of them all, of course, is the very specific injunction of Jesus in the Sermon on the Mount: "Be perfect, therefore, as your heavenly father is perfect" (Matt. 5:48). Such extensive and specific biblical teaching cannot be ignored or passed over lightly.

Obviously, the question that immediately rises is whether it is realistically possible for any finite human being to live up to such a standard. In most languages the word *perfect* is not a relative term; it is an absolute. There are no degrees or levels of perfection. Even the greatest egotist will readily admit that, no one is perfect. How, then, can a Christian be expected to measure up to such a standard or to be presumptuous enough even to claim to be able to live a life of perfection? To deal with this issue one needs to raise and find adequate answers to two basic questions. First, what is the true meaning of the word *perfect* as it is used in the New Testament? And second, how is it possible for a person really to live a holy life?

In seeking an answer to the first question it is important to keep in mind that all modern Bibles, except those in the original languages of Hebrew and Greek, are translations. Scholars who do the translating seek to find the words or phrases in the modern languages that best convey the meaning of the original. It is noteworthy that in several of the more recent translations of New Testament many of the passages that were earlier rendered using the word *perfect* now are translated with the word *mature*. For example:

1 Corinthians 2:6—"Speak a message of wisdom among the mature"; Ephesians 4:12-13, RSV— "Until we all attain . . . to mature manhood"; Colossians 1:28—"May present everyone perfect in Christ"; Colossians 4:12, RSV—"That you may stand mature and fully assured in all the will of God"; Hebrews 6:1—"Let us . . . go on to maturity." Obviously, several scholars feel that *mature* more adequately conveys the original meaning than does *perfect*.

It should be noted that this involves more than a choice between two words that mean essentially the same thing. *Mature* and *perfect* are not true synonyms. *Perfect* denotes flawlessness; *mature* means fully grown. It implies responsible adulthood, a readiness to fulfill the purposes for which one is created. To use the Pauline phrase quoted previously, it means being "fully assured in all the will of God." The "mature manhood" phrase in Ephesians (as noted previously) is defined by the writer as attaining "to the measure of the stature of the fullness of Christ." The change of words does not lower the standard or change the goal; it simply makes it more understandable.

Historically, even the most ardent advocates of Christian perfectionism have defined that term as equivalent to spiritual maturity. None have contended that perfection means absolute freedom from any human mistake or error. John Wesley, regarded as the father of the holiness movement, used the phrase "perfection of intention." By going further and defining sin as any *willful* transgression of God's law, he was able to speak of a life free from sin and "perfect" as to the intention of all one's behavior. The achievement of this purity of intentions he referred to as "perfect love."

Daniel S. Warner, a recognized leader in the nineteenth-century holiness movement and prominent among early leaders of the Church of God, was one of the strongest advocates of biblical holiness. In 1880 he wrote: "Perfection, as applied to redeemed souls, denotes the complete moral restoration of man from the effects of the Fall. Not physical or mental restoration, for that will not be until the Resurrection. . . . Christian perfection is, therefore, in *kind* and not in degree. In other words, it is the perfection of our moral nature, and not the development or full growth of our powers. . . . Hence perfection is the *state* of being *free* from sin" (*Bible Proofs of the Second Work of Grace,* p.28). He goes further to say that no one can claim perfection in degree, claiming to have reached the summit of Christian growth, "but thousands have received the Spirit's witness to perfect heart purity."

It thus becomes clear that when New Testament writers speak of perfection in Christ they mean spiritual maturity, perfect love, heart purity, victory over any intentional wrongdoing.

How Is This Possible?

The second of the basic questions, "How is it possible for a person really to live a holy life?" is easy to answer. Even in the framework of the definition of holy living just described it can be categorically declared, "Perfection in a moral sense is humanly impossible!" Through the centuries many people have tried—some very diligently—but all end up with the same experience the Apostle Paul reports about himself in the seventh chapter of Romans. In graphic language he relives the agony of his inner struggle. "In my flesh," he says, "I can will what is right, but I cannot do it" (v. 18, RSV). After further describing the struggle he voices his despair and cries, "What a wretched man I am! Who will rescue me from this body of death?" (v. 24). He just could not make himself a righteous person even though he desperately wanted it and tried diligently to achieve it.

The experience of Martin Luther, the great religious reformer of the sixteenth century, further illustrates the futility of trying to achieve righteousness through human effort. For many years he waged a vigorous struggle to overcome his own inclinations toward sin and to find peace of mind. He tried the way of withdrawing from worldly society by joining a monastic order. As a monk he went far beyond the demands of the Augustinian rule and engaged in prolonged periods of prayer and fasting. He spent long hours in pious meditation and contemplation. He even went to Rome and had an audience with the pope. None of these things brought him the assurance of peace with God that he so earnestly desired. Despite his great effort he was still, like Paul, a wretched man.

But God did not leave these men, or us,

without help in regard to this frustrating condition. He promised that the "pure in heart" would be "blessed" or happy (Matt. 5:8). He provided a way of escape from this wretchedness and Paul testifies that he found it. In verse 25 of that dismal seventh chapter of Romans he exalts, "Thanks be to God—through Jesus Christ our Lord." Martin Luther, likewise, found the inner assurance he sought through his discovery of the great truth of salvation by faith rather than works. This release from the power of sin, however, is only the beginning; God also provides the means for making the victory continuous. Jesus promised that he would send "another Counselor, to be with you forever, even the Spirit of truth . . . for he *dwells with* you, and *will be in* you" (John 14:16-17, RSV, italics added). One cannot imagine a helper with more complete availability—one who not only lives *with* us but actually is *in* us.

Receiving the Holy Spirit into one's life as a "helper" is a way of describing the experience of sanctification that has been so strongly emphasized in the Church of God and other holiness groups. The reality of continuous holy living is specifically declared by the Apostle Paul: "But now that you have been set free from sin and have become slaves to God, the benefit you reap leads to holiness, and the result is eternal life" (Rom. 6:22). Living a life completely under the direction of the Holy Spirit means living with victory over sinful desires and temptations. Paul makes it clear that such a life of holiness is expected of all followers of Christ: "For the grace of God that brings salvation has appeared to all men. It teaches us to say 'No' to ungodliness and worldly passions, and to live self-controlled, upright and godly lives in this present age, while we wait for the blessed hope—the glorious appearing of our great God and Savior, Jesus Christ, who gave himself, for us, to redeem us from all wickedness and to purify for himself a people that are his very own, eager to do what is good" (Titus 2:11-14).

A Holy Life-style

The doctrine of holiness is not just an abstract theological concept; it is a standard for everyday practical living. It is expressed in actions, attitudes, and aspirations. Paul admonished the Christians in Rome, "Do not be conformed to this world, but be transformed by the renewal of your mind" (Rom. 12:2, RSV). This nonconformity to the "world" relates to specific aspects of the prevailing culture. It may include abstaining from or even protesting against certain practices common in our society. It may mean a rejection of personal prestige or comfort. It may mean being regarded as a bit strange or peculiar. In the earlier days of the Church of God movement many "worldly" practices were to be avoided. The "saints" were warned against eating foods that might be harmful to their bodies, against dress that was immodest, gaudy, or extravagant, against personal adornment worn only for pride or show, against amusements that were degrading or a waste of time, and against participation in affairs of society that did not glorify God. For a period of time in the movement's history a great deal of attention was given to these dos and don'ts; they were regarded as a witness to the world that the people who claimed to be saints really were living a holy life. In more recent years less has been said about these specific rules and more emphasis has been given to the inner condition of the heart which prompts one's daily actions. Regardless of the emphasis, it must never be forgotten that holiness does not exist apart from behavior. Life-style is the real evidence as to whether or not the heart is pure.

Holiness is much more than the avoidance of worldliness, however; all of the "fruits" of the Spirit mentioned in Galatians 5:22-23 must loom large in all one's actions and relationships. As a witness to holiness nothing speaks louder than "love, joy, peace, patience, kindness, goodness, faithfulness, gentleness and self-control." We act out our holiness by relating in these ways to all people in our needy world.

The Spirit-filled Life

Being made holy by receiving the Holy Spirit into one's life does not produce a "pedestal" saint—a person so pious and sanctimonious that he or she has little relationship to the real world. It does, however, produce a person whose daily life evidences as least four very positive characteristics.

Victory—One of the best descriptions of the Spirit-filled life is Romans 6, the great victory chapter of the New Testament. Phrases like "no longer enslaved to sin," "dead to sin and alive to God," "brought from death to life," and "walk in newness of life" all denote that no longer do we need to go through the agony of fighting ourselves. "Perfect love casts out fear" (1 John 4:18, RSV). We have victory in Jesus. Through him we are "more than conquerors" (Rom. 8:37).

Growth—Victory over self frees us to grow in the grace and knowledge of our Lord Jesus Christ. The writer of Hebrews urges his readers to "go on to maturity" (6:1). To the Corinthians Paul wrote, "What we pray for is your improvement" (2 Cor. 13:9, RSV). Never in this life do we come to the end of this quest. Under the Spirit's guidance we, like Paul, keep pressing on "toward the goal," responding to the upward call of God in Christ Jesus (Phil. 3:14).

Power to witness—The last earthly words of Jesus proclaimed the promise that when his followers had been filled with the Holy Spirit they would have power and be public witnesses on a global scale to his work of salvation. A person who has been "perfected in Christ" cannot be silent about it. He or she is motivated to "Go, make disciples."

Tools for service—One of the bonuses in receiving the Holy Spirit is the bestowal of "gifts"—the "equipment" needed for effective service in the name of Christ. Gifts are given that we might glorify God with our bodies—serving human need, lifting the fallen, giving the cup of cold water, sharing our blessings, distributing the "fruit" of the Spirit to those who need these kinds of nourishment most.

Chapter 7

The Church—A Divinely Ordered Community

Biblical Resources

Matthew 16: 16-18; 18:19-20; 28:18-20
John 10:7-9
Acts 1:7-8; 2:46-47; 20:28
1 Corinthians 1:2; 12:18-20
Ephesians 1:22-23; 4:22-25
1 Timothy 3:5

For Study and Discussion

1. In what sense is the Church an institution? What characteristics would make the Church different from other institutions such as schools, businesses, governments, clubs, societies, or others?

2. What did Jesus mean when he said, "I will build my church?"

3. Make a list of the important meanings contained in the metaphor of the Church as "the body of Christ."

4. Give at least three reasons why the name of the church is an important issue.

5. All institutions require some rules and principles by which they operate. What are the really important principles for governing the Church?

6. How can "Holy Spirit leadership" actually be practiced in the life of a local congregation?

7. Is public worship a privilege or an obligation?

8. For what purposes does the Church exist?

Suggested Group Activity

Discuss why you go to church, especially this church. Identify which programs minister to you (and your family). What are some of the needs of members of the congregation that are not being met? What are some needs that are not being met for the people in your community? What new ministry programs should be developed?

Information and Issues

If any biblical teaching could be singled out as being most strongly emphasized in the Church of God movement it would have to be the doctrine of the Church. There is good reason for this. It was the dividedness and worldly mindedness of the church of their day which first awakened the early leaders of the movement to the need for reform. They understood the magnitude of the problem and realized that it could not be remedied even by massive external changes; it would be necessary to go to the Scriptures and discover again the real nature of Christ's desire and design for the Church. In their study they became aware of the centrality of the doctrine of the Church and recognized that in many ways all other Christian doctrines relate to and come to focus in the Church. It is in the Church that redeemed persons are brought together and function both individually and corporately as Christians. It is in the Church that Christian beliefs are articulated, taught, and practiced. It is primarily through the Church that Christian ministries and mission are carried out. It is the Church, the "bride of Christ," that the Lord will welcome to eternal life at the Last Judgment.

The early leaders of this reform movement often spoke of "seeing" the Church. By this they meant much more than simply understanding the meaning of a doctrine. They meant catching a "vision" of God's great plan for his people as a mighty company made up of all redeemed persons on the earth. They saw the Church as a fellowship that transcends all human barriers— race, color, nationality, caste, clan, class, sex, educational level, temperament, or culture. They saw the Church, brought together in the "bond of perfectness," as the most powerful witness to God's love for all humankind—a love also "shed abroad" in the hearts of his people and expressed in caring service. Such an insight was more than a profound concept; it was an exciting, possible reality. They believed it, they preached it, and they composed lyrics with music and sang it.

Why, then, should not this magnificent biblical teaching occupy a central place in the thought of a reform movement whose chief purpose was to proclaim and actualize the Church that Christ intended? Because of the importance of the doctrine of the Church in the life and witness of the Church of God, both this chapter and the next will be devoted to exploring the content of this grand vision.

God's Plan for His People

Even though the Church is primarily a fellowship it is also proper to refer to it as an institution since it is an established society. The Church, however, is unlike any other institution in the world. All other institutions—government, schools, business corporations, hospitals, service agencies, labor unions, professional societies, clubs, and any other structured groups of people—are humanly created and operated. Most institutions have worthy purposes and perform valuable functions in society. However, all except the Church have been humanly devised and have humanly defined reasons for existence. The Church is unique; it is a divine institution. Its members, of course, are people, but its origin, its name, its structure, and its purposes are divine. God is directly involved at every point. The New Testament makes it very clear that God intended there should be a continuing identity of his people and a framework within which they could function together. Important aspects of this divine plan include the following points.

1. *The Church is divine because it was founded by Jesus Christ and functions as his primary continuing living presence in the world.* Since the beginning of time God has had a "people." For many centuries his people primarily were those identified with the descendants of Jacob, the "children of Israel." With the coming of Christ, however, the offer of "chosenness" was extended to the whole human race and all who accepted the salvation made available by the death and resurrection of Jesus would become citizens of the "new Israel"— members of Christ's church. It was on this basis that Jesus could identify himself as the "founder" of the Church and promise its continuing witness in the world despite severe opposition—opposition even by "the gates of hell" (Matt. 16:18, KJV).

This primary relationship of Christ to the Church is repeatedly affirmed by the Apostle Paul. In his farewell speech to the Ephesian elders he instructs them to "be shepherds of the church of God, which he [Christ] purchased with his own blood" (Acts 20:28). In many of his letters Paul uses the image of the Church as the "body of Christ." This metaphor makes it possible to describe graphically many characteristics of the Church and to understand more adequately Christ's identity with it. Probably the most important meaning to be derived from this image is that the Church provides continuing visibility to the reality of the risen Savior. All that Jesus taught about himself, about the Father, about the continuing witness of the Holy Spirit, and about the ministry of those who would follow after him is realized and brought to focus in the Church. Many Christian theologians carry this Pauline thought a bit further and affirm: "The church is a continuation of Christ's incarnation."

Paul also uses the metaphor of the body to identify Christ's position in the Church. In Colossians 1:18 he writes: "And he is the head of the body, the church; he is the beginning and the firstborn from the dead, so that in everything he might have the supremacy." A similar affirmation is made in Ephesians 1:22-23: "And God placed all things under his feet and appointed him to be head over everything for the church, which is his body, the fullness of him who fills everything in every way." Without question, the Church is divine because Christ is the head.

In John 10:1-9 Jesus himself uses a metaphor to describe his function in the Church. In keeping with the image of himself as the "good shepherd," he refers to the company of his followers as a flock in a "sheepfold." In the context of this figure of speech he identifies his own role in the Church by declaring, "I am the gate; whoever enters through me will be saved. He will come in and go out and find pasture" (10:9). In speaking before the Jewish Sanhedrin the Apostle Peter is very explicit in affirming that Christ is the *only* door of entrance into the company of the redeemed. "Salvation," he says, "is found in no one else; for there is no other name under heaven given to men by which we must be saved" (Acts 4:12).

It thus becomes very evident that many sources in the New Testament affirm the divine nature of the Church because it was founded by Christ himself. Jesus continues to function as head of the Church and it is only through him that anyone can be admitted to membership in the Church.

2. *The church is divine because it is named for God the Father.* A name is important. In a family it signifies a person's primary relationship. In an institution it usually indicates both relationship and purpose. The name "Church of God" is more than a convenient label to put over the door of a place of worship. It is called the Church of God because it is God's church; it belongs to him. "Church of God" is the only name applied to the church in the New Testament. One exception is found in Romans 16:16 where "churches of Christ" is used, and here the reference obviously is to ownership rather than a title. This designation is specifically used twelve times and is implied in other references. It is used in all the senses that the term would be used in modern times. In several places, for instance, this name applies to the universal church, as in Acts 20:28 (feed the Church of God); 1 Corinthians 15:9 and Galatians 1:13 (persecuted the Church of God); 1 Corinthians

10:32 (Give no offense to the Church of God); 1 Corinthians 11:22 (Do you despise the Church of God?); and in 1 Timothy 3:5 (Take care of the Church of God). In other references it applies to the congregations in a geographic region, as in 1 Corinthians 11:16 and 1 Thessalonians 2:14 where the plural "Churches of God" is used. In still other places the term applies to local congregations, as in 1 Corinthians 1:2 and 2 Corinthians 1:1. Even more significant is the fact that Jesus prayed specifically (John 17:11-12) that his own followers be kept "in Thy name." Likewise, in Ephesians 3:14-15 there is reference to the whole family being named after the Father. Clearly "Church of God" is the name applied to the church in the New Testament; any other name is unnecessary and the use of other names can result only in dividing God's church.

We recognize that the use of this name in the modern world is not without problems. In the first place, many different unrelated groups, perhaps more than two hundred, use this name or some form of it. That makes identification of a particular group difficult and often may cause confusion or embarrassment. Then, too, some have said that it is arrogant to use this name since no congregation or group can live up to the perfection that the name implies. Others say that using this name is too idealistic and visionary. Even so, God's intention regarding a name for his people is plain; we must bear his name and honor it. No other name is suitable; no other name is so universal, so inclusive, so appropriate for people of all nations and races, and so expressive of the divine nature of the Church. In this name God is given the preeminence of which he alone is worthy. No one else, no system of polity, no single doctrine, no national designation or any other worldly label is good enough to be attached to the name of the Church. We can carry the name Church of God proudly, not arrogantly but humbly. It stretches us to live up to all that the name implies.

3. *The Church is divine because it is ruled and governed by the Holy Spirit.* Even though the New Testament documents contain many references to the Church, they provide little guidance for structuring this divine institution on earth. There are references to certain "offices" in the various churches—bishops, presbyters (elders), and deacons. There is no indication, however, that any of these were positions of authority. Rather, they identify certain functions and responsibilities of equal believer-members in each corporate body. Galatians 3:28, for example, notes the variety of people in the Church and then affirms, "You are all one in Christ Jesus." Even though there is no detailed blueprint for organizing the Church, the New Testament does set forth a *principle* for church government that is very clear. That principle is that all authority in the Church proceeds from Christ himself, functioning through the continuing presence and work of the Holy Spirit. This principle of Spirit-directed corporate function is

well set forth in 1 Corinthians 12. Paul writes, "There are different kinds of gifts, but the same Spirit. There are different kinds of service, but the same Lord. There are different kinds of working, but the same God works all of them in all men" (v. 4-6). "But in fact God has arranged the parts in the body, every one of them, just as he wanted them to be" (v. 18).

One of the most apparent themes in the early preaching of Church of God leaders was the proclamation of this principle. They strongly opposed all forms of humanly devised organization in the Church. They had a burning conviction that any attempt at "man-rule" was interference with the divine plan. Their real fear was not of organization itself but of humanly planned organization without dependence on the Holy Spirit. In order to allow this principle of divine rule to operate they resolved to develop no system of their own whatsoever. In each decision or function they sought the Spirit's guidance and acted in accordance with their leadings. For almost forty years the movement functioned in this context with very little structured organization.

As the movement became larger, however, it became apparent that much lost effort was being expended. There was duplication in some areas, neglect in others, and some confusion about who was responsible for what. The leaders came to realize that within the principle of Holy Spirit leadership they could and must organize their cooperative tasks in the Church. They discovered that in seeking to avoid human organization they had failed to remember that finite human beings, who work together, must have some commonly understood guidelines and responsibility designations if they are to attain their goals. Consequently, they began to plan together—plan for conserving gains that had been made, for teaching children and new converts in the meaning of the faith, for training leaders, and for the worldwide witness of the Church. While continuing to rejoice in the biblical truth that human beings cannot organize God's church, they also rejoiced in the discovery that the Holy Spirit can work through structures and in developing long-range plans as well as in immediate situations. It is important to remember the New Testament principle: the Church is not ours—it is God's. All persons and systems we use must be instruments that are open to the direction and guidance of the Holy Spirit.

The Church Is a Holy Community

As an institution the Church is divine; as an entity in human society, however, the Church is people. It is important to realize that the word *church* is never used to refer to an individual Christian; it applies only to a group of Christians in relationship to one another. Jesus said, "For where two or three come together in my name, there am I with them" (Matt. 18:20). Thus, the minimum is two. The Church, then, is God's people in community with one another. It is not buildings or offices, bishops or superintendents, rituals or symbols. It is not vestments or creeds. The Church is people—a special kind of gathered people with some special privileges and some special responsibilities.

1. The Church is a visible community of persons who, by God's grace, have been redeemed. The New Testament word *church* (*ecclesia* in the original Greek) means "called-out ones." It had been used in a secular sense to refer to any assembly of persons called together for some specific purpose. Jesus and the early Christians gave the word their own special meaning. They used it to refer to those who had been "called out" of their sinful condition and had been brought together into fellowship with Jesus Christ and with each other. The Church, thus, is composed only of those persons who have experienced salvation through Christ. To be redeemed is to be in the Church; that fact alone makes one a member.

Pioneer leaders of the Church of God movement were convinced that the various systems of church joining allowed many unworthy persons to become affiliated with a divine institution. In searching the Scriptures regarding qualifications and procedures for joining the Church they found only the simple affirmation that "the Lord added to the church daily such as should be saved" (Acts 2:47, KJV). It was apparent that this left no room for any human being to set the boundaries of the Church or to establish procedures for getting into it. In order to avoid the error of presuming to do God's judging for him, these reformers simply declared that all persons who had experienced the new birth were already members of the Church. No other initiation rite or ceremony was needed. As soon as one's sins are forgiven he or she enters the fellowship of the redeemed. The Church, then, is the visible community made up of all those in each place who can testify that this divine work has been accomplished in their own souls.

2. The Church is a worshiping, nurturing, and caring community. The Church is most visible when its members assemble at stated times to join in the worship and adoration of God. As voices are blended in hymns of praise, God is glorified and the hearts of the worshipers are edified. As individual and corporate prayers are lifted heavenward the faith of those assembled is also elevated. As the Word is proclaimed the meaning of the gospel brings renewed joy to believers and offers hope to sinners. As the Scriptures are read and expounded the minds of the hearers are enlightened and they are inspired to live their faith more boldly. As worshipers participate in the New Testament ordinances of the Lord's Supper and foot washing they express thanks to God and are brought into fellowship with all other Christians around the world. In worship, the Church appropriately and dramatically provides the communal setting for persons to respond to their need to adore God and to thank him for the great gift of his Son, Jesus Christ. Corporate worship is the sublimest expression of fellowship with God; it is one of the great privileges that accompanies participation in the community aspect of the Church. It is easy to understand why the writer of Hebrews would urge his readers, "Let us not

give up meeting together" (Heb. 10:25).

Members of the Church are also "members one of another" (Eph. 4:25). The Church is a sharing, caring, and burden-bearing fellowship. Its members help, encourage, and edify one another. The Church is a community of Christian concern and love.

3. The Church is a community on divine mission. The Church has a message to give to the world; its task is to serve the needs of the world. The message is that, in Christ, there is hope—hope for forgiveness of sin and release from guilt and shame, hope for empowerment to handle whatever life holds, and hope for a society where freedom and justice prevail. The task of the Church is to combine the word of reconciliation with the work of loving service. Love of neighbor is on the same level of importance as love for God. The Church on earth is indeed the "church militant"—the people of God taking the offensive against every form of evil. Loving service to those in need is the Christian way of letting one's "light" shine (Matt. 5:16). It is open evidence that God is at work among his people and in the world.

The mission of the Church is well summed up in the word *evangelization*. This involves both proclaiming and demonstrating the power of the gospel to the end that the world may believe. The imperative commands of the New Testament are plain and urgent—"Go, make disciples"; "Go into all the world"; "So send I you"; "You shall be my witnesses." For God's church, evangelizing is not an option; it is a necessary part of being the Church of God.

Chapter 8

The Church—A United Worldwide Community

Biblical Resources

Psalm 133:1
John 10:16; 17:20-21
Romans 12:4-5; 16:17-18
1 Corinthians 1:10-13; 12:13, 25
Galatians 3:26-29
Ephesians 4:3-6, 13
Colossians 3:12-14
Hebrews 2:11
1 Peter 3:8

For Study and Discussion

1. Christ's prayer recorded in John 17 was prior to Pentecost, the usually designated time for the beginning of the Church. What kind of unity do you think Jesus had in mind when he prayed "that all of them may be one?"

2. In their writings the apostles Paul and Peter have strong admonitions about preserving unity among Christians and issue warnings against division. If the first-century church is to be regarded as the ideal church, why was it necessary to give so much attention to the threat of disunity?

3. What are the greatest barriers to Christian unity in our own day? How can the experience of the early church assist in overcoming these barriers?

4. The Church of God movement has made Christian unity a central focus for its mission. What is being done by you and your congregation to make Christian unity a reality in your community?

5. How can one differentiate between "spiritual" unity and "invisible" unity? What are the reasons why one cannot accept invisible unity as the goal for God's church?

6. How is it possible to have real Christian unity and yet have diversity of theological viewpoints, preferences in worship patterns, or ideas about methodology?

7. Other national and international Christian groups are concerned also about the unity of the Church. What should be the relation of the Church of God movement to these groups?

Suggested Group Activity

Brainstorm what your local congregation could do to encourage Christian unity. Consider what might be done in your community and on a worldwide scope.

Information and Issues

The church is a dynamic institution. It is dynamic externally because it is a strong witness for righteousness in an evil world. It is dynamic internally because of its essential nature. The two aspects of the Church discussed in the previous chapter—its divine character and its human constituency—highlight the fact that within the Church two very powerful forces are put into tension with each other. The divine denotes holiness, unity, and all the infinite attributes of the Godhead; the human suggests imperfection, self-interest, and all the finite limitations of mortal persons. Placing these two unlike forces in the same context, as the Church does, aptly describes the exciting message of the gospel itself—the good news that God has made it possible for us human creatures to be elevated above our limitations and take on qualities of the Divine. What is true for individual redeemed persons is also true for the whole "realm of redemption," which is the Church. If the Church in the world is to be truly the "body of Christ," it also must take on corporately the qualities of the Divine. One of the most important of these qualities for the Church is unity—a quality that has been universally valued and sought. However, because of those very strong human factors, achievement of the goal has been very elusive throughout Christian history. Even with a unified structure until the eleventh century, there were always factions and dissident groups. Since the sixteenth century the disunity of the

Church has become more pervasive with little interest shown in changing the pattern of rivalry and competition. Until recent decades those calling for a renewed concern for restoring the unity of the Church have been "voices crying in the wilderness."

Biblical Basis

Over against the historical failure of the Church to maintain its unity there is the very extensive scriptural evidence that God wills the unity of all his people. Christ prayed earnestly for it. Leaders in the early church vigorously taught it and worked for it. The ancient psalmist expressed the beauty of God's intentional harmony among people when he wrote, "Behold how good and pleasant it is when brothers dwell in unity! It is like the precious oil upon the head. . . . It is like the dew of Hermon, which falls on the mountains of Zion!" (Ps. 133, RSV).

In the New Testament it may be noted first that there are many warnings against division, strife, and discord. In the list of "acts of the sinful nature" in Galatians 5:19-21, for example, more than half of the specific items mentioned relate to broken human relationships. In 1 Corinthians Paul makes division the first issue he attacks. "I appeal to you, brothers, in the name of our Lord Jesus Christ," he writes, "that all of you agree with one another so that there may be no divisions among you and that you may be perfectly united in mind and thought" (1 Cor.

1:10). Later, using the "body of Christ" metaphor for the Church, he affirms the truth that "God has combined the members . . . so that there should be no division in the body" (12:24-25). In the letter to the Romans he urges them "to watch out for those who cause divisions. . . . Keep away from them. For such people are not serving our Lord Christ, but their own appetites" (16:17-18).

Beyond these warnings against disunity there is a clear declaration about the basis of the unity that is advocated. It is not mere human unity that the inspired writers are talking about; it is unity in Christ. The Apostle Paul describes it well: "You are all sons of God through faith in Christ Jesus . . . you are all one in Christ" (Gal. 3:26-28). The writer of the Ephesian letter speaks of the "unity of the Spirit" and then equates the unity of the Church—the one body —with the unity of the Godhead itself. Exultantly he writes, "There is one body and one Spirit—just as you were called to one hope when you were called—one Lord, one faith, one baptism; one God and Father of all, who is over all and through all and in all" (Eph. 4:4-6). Such a concept follows precisely the deep desire expressed by Jesus shortly before his crucifixion. After praying specifically for his disciples he continued, "My prayer is not for them alone. I pray also for those who will believe in me through their message, that all of them may be one, Father, just as you are in me and I am in you. May they also be in us so that the world may believe that you have sent me" (John

17:20-21). The writer of Hebrews reaffirms this same message—the truth that unity with Christ unites one with all other participants in God's salvation. "Both the one who makes men holy and those who are made holy are of the same family. So Jesus is not ashamed to call them brothers" (Heb. 2:11).

The implications of this concept of unity are many. First and probably foremost is that the unity of all Christians is not just a goal to be sought; it is a given fact to be recognized and practiced. To be one with Christ is to be one with all others who are one with him. Paul affirms this very clearly: "Just as each of us has one body with many members, and these members do not all have the same function, so in Christ we who are many form one body, and each member belongs to all the others" (Rom. 12:4-5). The result of such relationships is a living community functioning in harmony with itself. The basic quality that makes this possible is love. The Apostle Peter puts harmony and love in proper perspective when he writes, "Finally, all of you, live in harmony with one another; be sympathetic, love as brothers, be compassionate and humble" (1 Pet. 3:8). Paul also speaks of clothing oneself in Christian virtues such as compassion, kindness, patience, and forgiveness—and then he adds, "And over all these virtues put on love, which binds them all together in perfect unity." To make it clear that he is talking about unity within the Church he adds, "Let the peace of Christ rule in your hearts, since as members of one body you were called to peace" (Col. 3:14-15).

Another very significant implication of this unity in Christ is that it overrides all the barriers that human society has erected that separate people from one another. Jesus himself projected the transcendence of these sociological obstacles to unity among his followers. In using the familiar "good shepherd" metaphor to describe his own role in God's plan, he also extended the borders of the Church far beyond Judaism by declaring, "I have other sheep that are not of this sheep pen. I must bring them also. They too will listen to my voice, and there shall be one flock and one shepherd" (John 10:16). To the then exclusivist Jewish people who prided themselves in their own "chosenness," this statement of Jesus was a bold announcement that God's redeeming love is not limited to a single group. It was his intention that all people who responded to his Word should be one flock.

Paul is even more extensive in naming the societal barriers that are overcome by Christ. To the Corinthians he wrote, "The body is a unit, though it is made up of many parts; and though all its parts are many, they form one body. So it is with Christ. For we were all baptized by one Spirit into one body—whether Jews or Greeks, slave or free—and we were all given the one Spirit to drink" (1 Cor. 12:12-13). In the Galatian letter he extends the list of barriers that are overcome in Christ to include sexual difference. Triumphantly he proclaims, "You are all sons of God through faith in

Christ Jesus, for all of you who were baptized into Christ have been clothed with Christ. There is neither Jew nor Greek, slave nor free, male nor female, for you are all one in Christ Jesus" (Gal. 3:26-28).

There really is no end to the catalog of cultural and social obstructions to fellowship and unity that are surmounted in Christ. Whether it be differences in race, nationality, class, economics, color, language, or political persuasion, in Christ all of these are conquered and all of God's daughters and sons are united in one body.

Church of God Commitment to Unity

The strong emphasis on the doctrine of the Church by the Church of God movement has already been noted. Without question the most prominent aspect of the emphasis has been on the unity of the Church. A study of the history of this movement reveals that both its original and continuing reason for existence focuses conspicuously on challenging the denominational system that divides the Church and on proclaiming the biblical teachings on Christian unity. The leaders of the movement, from the earliest beginnings to the present, have decried the "Babel confusion" of a divided church. At the same time, they also proclaimed the vision of a full restoration of the oneness of God's church with biblical truth as its only creed and holiness as its most evident characteristic. The movement's leadership has declared over and over again that a primary aspect of this group's mission is to call the whole church to judgment regarding its divided state, to lift up the scriptural standard of Christian unity, and to exhibit in its own existence the reality of a visible worldwide fellowship in which the only criterion for membership is testimony that one is a redeemed child of God.

To these religious reformers this "light" on the significance of the unity of the Church has been more than the rediscovery of a basic biblical doctrine or just the projection of a utopian dream. The movement has gone beyond simply deploring the shame of a divided church and has sought to focus on a solution to the problem. That solution, basically, has been seen as a willingness to abandon the entrenched human-made sectarian systems that have separated Christians from one another. Then, following the minimal patterns of structure suggested in the New Testament, it is necessary to place the direction of the corporate affairs of the Church completely in the hands of the Holy Spirit. When this obviously simplistic approach to Christian unity was propounded in the late nineteenth century its potential results were immediately apparent. The concept soon began to generate considerable excitement and the early leaders of the movement enthusiastically proclaimed their vision of a united and holy church of God.

The zeal of these "flying messengers" was expressed in many ways. By sermons, songs, and hundreds of printed pages they declared that the "church triumphant" need not wait for a new age to be revealed; it was becoming a present reality. Lustily they sang,

> There's a mighty reformation sweeping o'er the land,
> God is gathering his people by his mighty hand.

and,

> From all the divisions in which they were scattered,
> Thy children are gathering home.

Another lyric affirmed:

> The day of sects and creeds for us forevermore is past,
> Our brotherhood are all the saints upon the world so vast;
> We reach our hands in fellowship to every blood-washed one,
> While love entwines about each heart in which God's will is done.

Beyond these jubilant affirmations there was clear and solid scriptural teaching about the nature of a united church. Jesus Christ founded only one church; it is composed of all persons who have experienced redemption in Christ; its faith is based on the whole Word of God; it is ruled by the Holy Spirit. These basic theological concepts were also lyricized and congregations witness to these truths as they sing, "I'm Redeemed . . . and I'm walking in the light," "Back to the Blessed Old Bible," and "How Sweet This Bond of Perfectness." They saw the one Church of God, and they knew it was not theirs to construct or organize; a united church was not something to be fashioned by any human process. Real unity comes only as the gift of God and is an expression of his love. As Daniel S. Warner put it, "O brethren how this perfect love unites us all in Jesus! One heart, and soul, and mind we prove the union heaven gave us."

But There Are Barriers

The loftiness of the vision of Christian unity must not blind one, however, to the practical difficulties in reaching such a goal. The barriers are very great and very complex. Many of these divisive differences have existed for centuries. Until relatively recent time the divisions between Christians were identified as being primarily doctrinal with the various viewpoints being propounded by the many separate denominations. This competitive situation within Christianity does exist and has accelerated in the last two centuries. Denominational distinctives often foster such strong loyalties that rivalry between groups may become very intense and even bitter. The general acceptance, since the sixteenth century, of the denominational system has made it possible for persons differing with the prevailing beliefs or practices of a particular group to move out of that group and start a new one. The ease with which this dividing can take place has produced more than three hundred separated groups of Christians, most of which originated in Europe and America and have been exported to other parts of the world. Despite many mergers in recent years, these divisions still constitute the most extensive and visible aspect of Christian disunity.

There are other kinds of barriers to unity, though, that are just as great—or even greater. Particularly during the last century, Christians have grouped themselves under certain theological labels and engage in verbal battle with all who disagree. Some identify themselves as being conservative, some liberal, and some moderate. Some are extremists in all of these categories. Such divisions cut across denominational lines and sometimes produce splits in denominations or within congregations. Almost any group has to deal with factions and threat of fragmentation.

There are also barriers between Christians that have very little to do with theology. Such things as differences in social status (class), economic resources (wealth), or culture (level of education, life-style, and so on) often separate people from one another even though they profess faith in Jesus Christ. Then, too, there are many psychological factors that produce barriers—personality differences, rivalries for recognition and position, and just plain misunderstandings and faulty interpretations. All of these are very real enemies of unity that affect all of human society as well as the Church.

One of the most devastating of the nonreligious barriers that separate Christians from one another is that of differences in race and nationality. Prejudices regarding skin color, racial background, and national allegiance are deeply engrained in all societies. These are very difficult to overcome. It has already been noted that in Christ all these differences are overcome, but the human factor is still present. Deliberate and sometimes painful application of the Christian gospel to these societal problems is required if real unity is to be achieved. This is one area in which the Church in almost every part of the world still has a great unfinished task. Many Christian groups remain separated from one another along the lines of race, color, and nationality.

Indeed, Christian disunity is a very great and complex problem. There are no easy or automatic solutions to it.

The Possible Dream

Despite the difficulties, any sincere Christian can never forget that oneness in Christ is the clear and positive teaching of the whole New Testament. There is no way to ignore the stated intention of Christ for the unity of his followers or the repeated admonitions of the apostolic writers to maintain the unity of the faith. The early leaders of the Church of God movement were especially impressed by this message. They were captivated by the vision of one holy church. They were committed to proclaim it in spite of the seemingly impossible barriers that would have to be overcome. Even though no detailed blueprint for a united church has been drawn, there are three major aspects of Christian unity that have been envisioned as being both scriptural and practical.

1. Unity is essentially spiritual. It is grounded in the common identity of all who are "in Christ." This means that it cannot be devised or fashioned by human effort. Denominational mergers, federations or councils of churches, and ecumenical dialogue may be helpful and desirable. But only participation in Christ can surmount the human and social barriers that separate people from one another.

2. Unity must be visible. It is not enough to say, as some do, that all Christians are spiritually one even though they are divided into separated denominations and sects. These divisions are negative evidence to the power of God's love. They are contrary to Christ's intention for the Church. Real Christian unity must become visible by the absence of competitive divisions in the body of Christ. It must be visible at all levels—local, regional, and universal.

3. Unity is the springboard for service and witness. Christian unity is not an end in itself. Jesus stated this very clearly: "I pray that all of them may be one . . . so that the world may believe." Division hinders, distorts, and often destroys the witness of the Church to the redeeming work of Christ. Worldwide unity is the ultimate goal toward which God is leading the Church.

Chapter 9

Christian Ordinances

Biblical Resources

General:	Matthew 28:20
Baptism:	Matthew 3:13-17; 28:19
	Mark 16:15-16
	John 4:1-2
	Acts 2:38, 41; 3:19; 8:12, 39; 22:16
	Romans 6:1-4
	Galatians 2:20
	Colossians 2:12
	1 Peter 3:21
Communion:	Matthew 26:26-28
	Mark 14:22-24
	Luke 22:19-20
	Acts 20:27
	1 Corinthians 10:16-17; 11:20, 23-26

Foot Washing: John 13:1-17 (especially v. 14-15)
1 Timothy 5:9-10

For Study and Discussion

1. Why are symbols and celebrations important for (1) individual persons, (2) families, (3) groups, (4) nations?

2. What are the dangers inherent in the use of symbols, rites, and ceremonies?

3. What is the difference between an "ordinance" and a "sacrament?" In which category would the practices instituted by Jesus fall?

4. According to scriptural teaching, who is eligible to be baptized? Which mode of baptism is taught in the New Testament? Why have other modes become prevalent in Christian practice? List the basic meanings that are symbolized in baptism.

5. Why is the word *Eucharist* often used in describing the observance of the Lord's Supper? Why is it also called "Holy Communion?" What are the implications of the phrase "in remembrance of me," as it is used in a communion service?

6. Why do relatively few Christian groups practice the ordinance of foot washing? Why is it important for the Church of God to continue observing this ordinance?

Suggested Group Activity

Invite your pastor to lead your group in a worship service in which you can experience the ordinances. It may be that some in your group have never been baptized.

Information and Issues

Ceremony and celebration are an important part of human existence. Every culture, from the most simple to the most sophisticated, has its special rites and ceremonies. At these times they recognize and celebrate certain days, seasons, events, persons, customs, or beliefs that have significant meaning for particular groups of people. Some groups may be small, such as families; other groups may be larger, such as tribes or nations. Still other groups may be global in scope, such as the worldwide religions, which are universal in their constituency. This multitude of groups utilizes ritual, ceremony, and symbolic action for a wide variety of purposes: commemorating, emphasizing, teaching, preserving, honoring, celebrating, remembering, petitioning, purifying, affirming, initiating, terminating, and so on. Rites and ceremonies have been especially important in the practice of religion. All of the world's systems of faith, from the most primitive animism to the most complex universal religions, have developed and use ritualistic practices as one of the means for accomplishing their purposes. Christianity is no exception. From its earliest beginning the Church has utilized symbols, ceremonies, and ritualistic practices to convey meanings that are important to understanding and propagating faith in Jesus as the Christ.

Christian Observances

In general, it can be said that Christianity is less ritualistic than most other religions since its primary emphasis is faith in the divine Christ rather than any expectation to accomplish something through the performance of certain ceremonial acts. There are three observances that fall in the category of having been done by Jesus himself. These are followed by his request that those who would accept his teaching should do also. They are baptism, the Lord's Supper, and foot washing. The repetition of these observances was practiced by the early Christians and has been perpetuated, in various forms and degrees, by the Church through the centuries.

The first two of these observances, baptism and the Lord's Supper, have been and are practiced by nearly all Christians. (A few groups, such as the Quakers, reject all outward ceremonial acts as being mere substitutes for inner spiritual experience, and so they practice none of these rites.) Only a small number of groups, however, practice the third of these observances—foot washing. The Church of God movement is one of these. Yet, there are many variant understandings of the meaning of these three practices and the manner in which they should be performed. In fact, disagreement among Christians regarding the Lord's Supper has often have been described as "our deepest difference," and constitutes the greatest doctrinal barrier to Christian unity. It becomes very important, then, to review again the biblical basis for observing these ceremonies and to understand the Christian meanings that they symbolize.

Before discussing each of these practices it will be of value to note that various Christian groups use two different words to designate these ceremonial acts. Some refer to them as "sacraments"; others call them "ordinances." There is considerable difference in the meaning between these two words. The word *sacrament* refers to a sacred or holy act. By implication the very performance of such an act is considered to effect a designated spiritual result. Hence, the act itself is considered to be "efficacious" for salvation, protection from evil, or some other desired spiritual blessing. This would mean, for instance, that the very act of being baptized would result in forgiveness from sin or that partaking of the bread and wine in communion would mean that Christ actually had been taken into one's body and life. The word *ordinance,* on the other hand, means a divine admonition or command—acts that Christ said should or ought to be repeated. The performance of these acts is a response to that command and a witness to one's obedience to Christ. The act itself does not produce the result but is a public testimony that a spiritual work has already been accomplished in one's life through Christ's death and resurrection.

For leaders in the Church of God movement the difference between these two words is very significant, entailing an important theological distinction. The sacramental view suggests the possibility of salvation by "works" (i.e. the performance of certain acts); the ordinance view preserves the concept of salvation by faith, with works following. Consequently, the ordinance interpretation has been regarded as the teaching of the New Testament. Even though the word *sacrament* might sometimes be used in reference to one of these acts, its use is nontechnical and its intended meaning would be the same as *ordinance*.

Baptism

Many religions have rituals signifying a cleansing or purification. Often this is accomplished by a ceremonial washing with water or oil. The Jews, for instance, considerably earlier than the time of Christ, required that converts from pagan religions must not only be circumcised but also must be immersed completely in water in order to be cleansed from their former defilement. John the Baptizer preached that wayward Jews also should repent of their sins and be baptized in the same manner as Gentile converts. It was to this radical preacher of repentance and holiness that Jesus went and requested baptism for himself (Matt. 3:13-17; Mark 1:9-11; Luke 3:21-22). For Jesus, baptism was not for repentance but was a symbol of his sinless life. It was a public witness that God the Father had sent his Son for a very special mission and ministry. Not only was Jesus himself baptized but he also asked his disciples to baptize those who became his followers (John 4:1-2). Then, just before he ascended into heaven, Jesus declared, "Therefore go and make disciples of all nations, baptizing them in the name of the Father and of the Son and of the Holy Spirit" (Matt. 28:19). There is no command of Jesus that is more explicit than that of Christian baptism.

As noted earlier, most Christians accept the necessity of heeding this command, and so baptism is not a disputed doctrine. There are, however, great varieties in the understandings of the meaning of baptism and the manner of administering this important Christian rite. Although all differences cannot be noted, there are at least three important questions to which biblical answers must be sought if one is to properly understand and practice this ordinance.

1. Who is eligible to be baptized? It is clear that the biblical documents support the view that Christian baptism is for believers only. Most references to baptism in the New Testament are preceded by the words *repent* and/or *believe,* indicating that these are prerequisites for baptism. In Peter's sermon at Pentecost, for instance, he declared, "Repent and be baptized, every one of you, in the name of Jesus Christ so that your sins may be forgiven" (Acts 2:38). Jesus himself affirmed, "Whoever believes and is baptized will be saved, but whoever does not believe will be condemned" (Mark 16:16). In the Acts 8:12 account of Philip's preaching it is reported: "But when they believed . . . they were baptized, both men and women." Without doubt the early church practiced believers' baptism.

Such a procedure, however, left open a very

important question: what is the spiritual state of young children who might die before they were able to give their own conscious response to the gospel? Obviously an infant is not aware of sin, and so he or she cannot repent and is too young to "believe on the Lord Jesus Christ." In dealing with this issue it came to be noted that some New Testament references to baptism could possibly include children, such as the "household" of the jailer at Philippi (Acts 16:33). Later, the first-century Christian scholars, in the context of a sacramental view of baptism, began to develop the teaching that infants could be baptized. Thus, they obtained remission from the guilt of original sin, assuring salvation if the child died in infancy. This doctrine came to be accepted in the Roman and Eastern Orthodox churches and has been continued in many Protestant groups. While providing reassurance for concerned parents, such teaching really has no basis in Scripture. In regard to the original question it should be noted that the spiritual state of infants seems not to have been a questionable issue for Jesus or the early Christians. Had not the Master gathered the children around him and lovingly declared, "Of such is the kingdom of heaven" (Matt. 19:14, KJV)?

2. What is the biblical mode of baptism? The New Testament Greek word *baptizo* means to "immerse, dip, or plunge." Consequently, biblical and historical scholars agree that Jesus' disciples and the early church baptized converts

by immersion only. Baptism by affusion (pouring) and sprinkling water on the candidate came later as accommodations to convenience and cultural preference. Exceptions to immersion were first made for those who were feeble or ill. Still later the baptism of infants was initiated and the Roman Catholic church abandoned the practice of immersion. Most Protestant churches continued the practice of infant baptism and used the mode of either sprinkling or pouring. Some Eastern Orthodox churches and several Protestant groups, however, have upheld the concept of believers' baptism and have insisted that baptism by immersion is the only mode that is biblical and that it symbolizes the full meaning of this religious rite. The Church of God movement is among those who uphold this viewpoint.

3. What is symbolized in baptism by immersion? At least three obvious significant meanings are conveyed in the act of baptism by this mode: (a) Cleansing. The outward cleansing of the whole body is a visual ceremonial testimony that an inner cleansing of the whole self has taken place. Texts that might seem to support the idea of "baptismal regeneration" must be interpreted in this context. In the often quoted 1 Peter 3:21 passage, for instance, the main point is not the phrase "baptism that now saves you," but the latter part of the verse, "the pledge of a good conscience toward God." Likewise, in Acts 22:16 the command of Ananias to Saul, "Get up, be baptized, and wash your sins away," was given after Saul had received his

sight and had acknowledged his call to be a witness for Christ. Baptism is thus a symbol of forgiveness, which is a cleansing from the guilt of sin. (b) Identity with Christ's death and the burial of sin. This is another way of symbolizing the atoning work of Christ and the end of sin's power in one's life. It is beautifully phrased by Paul in Romans 6:1-4: "All of us who were baptized into Christ Jesus were baptized into his death." In Colossians 2:12 the Apostle uses the same metaphor and speaks of "being buried with him in baptism." Baptism by immersion is thus a meaningful symbol of the "burial" of the power of sin made possible by the death of Christ. (c) Resurrection to "newness of life." In these same biblical passages there is the further symbolism of resurrection—coming up out of the water as Christ arose from the grave. Thus, like the Ethiopian eunuch, the baptized person can go "on his way rejoicing" (Acts 8:39), having witnessed to the world the experience of being a redeemed person.

The Lord's Supper

Sacred meals or feasts are a part of the ritual observances in many religions. The Jews made extensive use of foods in the celebration of their holy occasions. In fact, it was immediately following the observance of the Feast of the Passover that Jesus instituted the rite of the Lord's Supper. The story of this event is recorded in four different places in the New Testament—Matthew 26:26-28; Mark 14:22-24; Luke 22:19-20; 1 Corinthians 11:23-30. The latter reference is the earliest and most complete of these written accounts. The expectation that there should be continued observance of this ceremony is indicated by Jesus' request: "Do this . . . in remembrance of me. For whenever you eat this bread and drink this cup, you proclaim the Lord's death until he comes" (1 Cor. 11:25-26). It is thus clear that Jesus expected his followers to repeat this observance until his return to the earth. This indeed has happened, for this rite was practiced in the early church and has been widely observed by Christians ever since.

This observance is referred to by three different names. In 1 Corinthians 10:16-17 the terms *eucharist* ("cup of thanksgiving") and *communion* (the communion of the body of Christ) are both used. In one place, 1 Corinthians 11:20, the rite is referred to as "the Lord's Supper." Thus all three terms are used widely in the Church and all are proper; each gives special emphasis to various aspects of the observance.

The symbolism of this simple ceremony is drawn from one event—the death of Jesus on the cross. In the everyday act of eating and drinking Jesus brought together and highlighted the great messages of incarnation, sacrifice, atonement, redemption, thanksgiving, and fellowship. Put more systematically, one can note at least four significant spiritual messages that are conveyed in the observance of this ordinance.

1. It is a memorial. The words "Do this in remembrance of me" are primary. Participation in the Lord's Supper is a continuing reminder of the sacrificial death of Christ and the redemp-

tive love of God that it represents. The two elements, bread and wine, become very specific reminders of the magnitude of that sacrifice—the broken body, the spilled blood. To partake of the elements is to remember Jesus and the great gift he gave us.

2. It is a thanksgiving. The aspect of thanks looms large in this rite. Jesus not only blessed the elements but he also offered the "cup of blessing." Eucharist is a most appropriate designation for this observance. Beyond remembering, participation in the Supper impels one to express deep thanks to God for the great gift of his Son.

3. It is a proclamation. The statement "You proclaim the Lord's death until he comes" identifies the evangelistic purpose of the Supper. The public observance of this memorial is a witness to the world of one's faith in the atoning work of Christ. It is testimony to personal participation in the redemption that Jesus offers. For this reason, only persons who can give such a testimony should participate. The Eucharist is a proclamation of the gospel.

4. It is a communion. There are two important involvements in this aspect of the Supper. First, there is participation in the suffering of Christ, thus entering into communion with him. Then there is the corporate involvement as one participates alongside other redeemed persons, thus expressing the unity of all God's people at the "table of the LORD." It is a witness to the oneness and equality of all the redeemed, a

testimony that all who confess Christ as Savior are in communion with God and with one another.

Unfortunately, the Eucharist also has been an occasion for much controversy and disagreement among Christians. Because of its obvious importance, various groups have established precise rules for administering this observance and have developed their own theological interpretations of its meaning. At least four widely held viewpoints, which are not supported by Scripture, should be identified and rejected.

1. Transubstantiation. This view, developed in the ninth century, holds that in the act of blessing the elements the bread actually becomes the flesh of Christ and the wine his blood. The participant would thus take Christ, literally, into his or her own body. Such a view negates the remembrance aspect of the Supper and defines its value in physical rather than spiritual terms.

2. Sacrificing Christ anew. To "proclaim the Lord's death" is not an injunction to repeat it. The Supper is not a sacrifice. In the words of the writer of Hebrews, "Christ was sacrificed once to take away the sins of many people" (9:28).

3. Efficacious in itself. This sacramental view would hold that partaking of the elements of the Supper would produce such spiritual values as forgiveness and redemption even without repentance. Such an interpretation is inconsistent with all other basic teachings of the New Testament.

4. Valid only when "properly" administered. In prescribing precise regulations regarding who may "celebrate" communion and the ritual that must be followed, many groups go far beyond the scriptures in restricting the invitation to the Lord's table. Such limitations as "close" communion and requiring the celebrant to be in the line of "apostolic succession" certainly are not biblical.

The variety of opinions regarding the frequency of this observance—ranging from daily to annual—are really not crucial. There is no biblical guidance regarding this matter, so it would appear to be an optional preference. Most congregations in the Church of God movement, for instance, would observe the Lord's Supper at least quarterly. Some groups observe it each week. The really important thing is to observe it with reverence and meaning.

Foot Washing

As already noted, this ordinance is not as widely practiced as the other two. Even so, it has a clear basis in Scripture. In John 13:1-17 there is the detailed account of Jesus' washing the feet of his disciples. At the conclusion of this act Jesus said to them, "Now that I, your Lord and Teacher, have washed your feet, you also should wash one another's feet. I have set you an example that you should do as I have done for you" (v. 14-15).

The only biblical evidence that this ordinance was practiced in the early church is 1 Timothy 5:10 where "washing the feet of the saints" is cited as one of the qualifications of a needy widow in order to participate in the food distribution. This could refer to the ordinance of foot washing but it also could mean simply that she must have shown hospitality to persons from the church who visited her home, since that would be an expected amenity in the culture of that day.

Despite this scanty evidence it is not possible to ignore the very specific command of Jesus. It is on this basis that foot washing has taken its place among the ordinances. Although it has not been widely practiced, there has not been a time in Christian history when the rite has not been observed by some group. In the sixteenth century there was a revival of this ordinance by several of the groups identified with the radical reformation. The early leaders of the Church of God reform movement of the nineteenth century also read this command of Jesus and began practicing foot washing as an ordinance. In the Church of God the practice of foot washing has never been a "test of fellowship." Thus, if some congregations either in America or other parts of the world do not observe this rite it poses no problem.

Those who participate in a service of foot washing find it a very meaningful experience. In addition to the satisfaction of having followed the Lord's command, there are two great meanings symbolized in this act:

1. Humility. Jesus performed this act immediately after some of his disciples had quarreled

about which of them would be the greatest. Washing their feet was really a rebuke to their arrogance and desire for high position. By this example he demonstrated what he had taught them earlier: he that would be great among you let him be a servant.

2. Service. Serving the needs of fellow human beings is one of the important aspects of the Christian message. The servant image was accepted by Jesus; it is appropriate that it also apply to his followers. Washing another person's feet symbolizes the servant role that every Christian should follow.

In observing any or all of these ordinances it is important to keep in mind that in and of themselves they may be nothing but empty ceremonies. But when they are practiced in obedience to Christ and for the purposes he designed, they become a means to make living the gospel the most significant aspect of human existence. The last earthly words of Jesus give this call to obedience—as well as this promise: "Teaching them to observe all things whatsoever I have commanded you: and lo, I am with you alway, even unto the end of the world" (Matt. 28:20).

Chapter 10

Divine Physical Healing

Biblical Resources

Psalm 103:1-3
Isaiah 35:5-6; 42:6-7; 53:4-5; 61:1
Malachi 4:2
Matthew 8:16-17; 9:1-2, 35-36; 10:1, 7-8; 14:14;
17:19-20
Mark 1:41; 5:18-20; 6:12-13; 16:17-18
Luke 4:18-21; 10:9
John 14:12-13
Acts 3:1-11; 5:12-16
Romans 8:23
1 Corinthians 12:4-11, 28-30
James 4:3; 5:14-16

For Study and Discussion

1. What are some Old Testament references that indicate that the Jewish people linked physical health to their faith?

2. Explain why healing would be included so prominently in many of the prophetic affirmations of the messianic hope.

3. What distinction should be made between the term *divine healing* and the healing processes of nature that are divinely ordered?

4. What are the basic theological foundations for belief in miraculous healing of the human body?

5. The ministry of Jesus and his disciples included many instances of healing. Does this warrant the continuation of this aspect of Christian ministry today? Why?

6. Assess the view that healing is included in Christ's atonement for sin.

7. There are many "faith healers" found today among some popular TV preachers and strange cults. What should be one's attitude toward such "healers?"

8. Does "trusting in the Lord" for healing rule out the seeking of medical assistance?

9. What are one's personal responsibilities for maintaining and improving his or her own health and physical fitness?

Suggested Group Activity

It may be that some persons in your group have experienced personally, or have observed someone else's healing. Share these experiences.

Information and Issues

Most of the religious systems of the world include some teaching or practice that relates to physical healing. Even the most primitive religions have charms, potions, incantations, or other devices that promise to preserve physical health or cure diseases. Many groups have professional healers, such as medicine men or shamans, who are believed to have power for healing sicknesses or have some control over the unseen spirits that bring affliction. Such religious involvement obviously is based on the belief that disease and suffering are caused by invisible forces. This may be either evil spirits, which must be exorcised or overcome, or good spirits that have become displeased or angry. In either case some religious procedure is devised either to drive away or to appease the cause of the problem. Often this would involve some sacrificial rite or other act of penance. In many of the major religions there are holy places such as temples, shrines, and fountains to which afflicted persons may go to be cured. Throughout human history healing has been closely associated with religious faith.

In Judaism, the cradle of Christianity, there was little of this "pagan" approach to physical healing. There were basic concepts, however, which defined some specific relationships between the Hebrew faith and physical health. For example, the Jews strongly believed the following things: (1) God both causes and allows sickness and suffering to come upon people in order to accomplish his higher purposes. The plagues that were brought upon Egypt, and the many instances when suffering was meted out to Israel as punishment for disobedience, would be examples of affliction caused by God. The story of Job would be an instance when God allowed disease and disaster to come upon one of his followers in order to demonstrate the faithfulness of a committed servant. (2) God can and does heal persons in miraculous ways. Psalm 103 exultantly declares, "Praise the Lord, O my soul, and forget not all his benefits. He forgives all my sins and heals all my diseases." Even though the Old Testament does not cite a multitude of instances of divine healing, there are some significant ones. The stories of Naaman (2 Kings 5) and Hezekiah (2 Kings 20) would be examples. (3) There is a close relationship between physical well-being and obedience to God. The terms of the covenant promised blessings and prosperity for obedience and threatened curses, including "wasting disease, with fever and inflamation," for disobedience (Deut. 28). (4) Healing is an important benefit to be realized with the coming of the promised Messiah. Isaiah 35:5-6 and 42:7, for instance, speak of opening the eyes of the blind. Chapter 53 explicitly declares, "He took up our infirmities and carried our sorrows . . . and by his wounds we are healed" (vv. 4-5). The Isaiah 61:1 passage, which proclaims, "He has sent me to bind up the brokenhearted," was quoted and claimed by Jesus in announcing his messiahship (Luke 4:18-20). Malachi says that on the day of the Lord "the sun of righteousness will rise with healing in its wings" (4:2). Jesus, as the promised Messiah, certainly had good reason to make healing a major aspect of his earthly ministry.

Divine Healing: The Problem of Definition

In the strictest sense, all healing is divine. Doctors, including surgeons, psychiatrists, therapists, and others, cannot heal; they can only help to create conditions that enable natural healing to take place. Medicines, including miracle drugs, cannot heal; they can only assist the body in fighting the cause of the disease. God, as creator, built into the human body the necessary mechanisms to maintain health. The body has the ability to fight disease and to recover from even very severe injuries. So God is involved in all healing, whether with or without incidental assistance by doctors or medicine.

The term *divine healing* is not used in a technical sense to describe the obviously natural healing of disease, injury, or disfunction. Neither is it used in reference to healing assisted by doctors or medicines. As commonly understood, divine healing relates only to a miraculous cure—a healing that cannot be explained in any way other than divine intervention. It means healing that results solely from prayer and the exercise of faith without resort to any human aids or remedies. It is with this understanding that the subject is now explored—historically, theologically, biblically, and practically.

Healing in Christian History and in the Church of God

Divine healing, thus defined, has been taught and practiced throughout Christian history by at least some segments of the universal church.

At various times, however, some Christian groups have slipped into near pagan practices by attaching healing powers to designated holy relics, such as skeleton parts or possessions of well-known martyrs or saints. In many instances shrines have been erected at places associated with these "holy" persons. These have become the location for reported miracles and healings. Such practices, of course, are far removed from the healings described in the New Testament. Fortunately, there have also been those who continued the practice of healing by prayer and faith.

In recent times there has been a revival of interest in divine healing. Some of this new emphasis is biblical and wholesome; some of it is a gross distortion. Many cultic groups advocate various forms of mental healing—stressing the power of mind over matter. Others identify certain persons as professional healers, claiming they have special access to the power of God. Using the New Testament as a guide, one must learn to distinguish between the authentic and the false.

Since its beginning, the Church of God movement has recognized divine physical healing as a biblical doctrine and has practiced anointing and prayer for the sick. Largely under the influence of *Gospel Trumpet* editor Enoch E. Byrum, who claimed the gift of "faith for healing," this emphasis was very prominent during the first quarter of the twentieth century. Some leaders taught that trusting God was the only suitable method for Christians to deal with sickness and injury; doctors, medicines, and hospitals were to be avoided. In later years this "trusting even to death" position has been generally modified, allowing for sound human judgment in utilizing whatever aids to health medical science has developed. At the same time there has been perhaps an even stronger emphasis on prayer for the sick and exercising faith in God's power to heal and willingness to perform miracles. Without fanfare or spectacular demonstrations, prayer for the sick and testimonies of healing continue to be an important aspect of teaching and practice in the Church of God. There are good reasons for maintaining this emphasis.

Divine Healing Is Theologically Sound

The theological foundation for this doctrine is rooted in a proper understanding of the nature of God. Three aspects are evident.

1. God is creator. As the maker of the universe and all that is in it, including the human species, it is only logical that God's knowledge and ability would also include the means to repair, correct, restore, and protect this creation. Obviously God planned this from the beginning, for there are highly efficient protective and restorative processes built into every human body. Should some of these systems be damaged or overpowered, who would know what to do better than the maker himself?

2. God is all-powerful. God's knowledge and power are wonderfully demonstrated in the mul-

titude of orderly systems that function in all his creation. This does not mean that God limits action to these "natural" laws. God is omnipotent; miracles are not out of character for him. Miraculous divine healing is one way God reminds us of his unlimited power. In Jesus' day, and in our own time, healings often become a means for convincing unbelievers that God is indeed God, the all-powerful ruler of the universe.

3. God is love. Throughout the Bible, God's love and concern for humankind is emphasized. This is most evident in the healing ministry of Jesus. So many of the Gospel accounts of these incidents include the phrase "He was moved with compassion" (Matt. 9:35-36; 14:14; Mark 1:41; 5:18-20). Had Jesus wanted only to demonstrate his supernatural power he could have performed miracles much more spectacular than healing ordinary people of the common diseases of that day. The miracles of Jesus were acts of mercy and helpfulness; they were evidences of God's love. So, indeed, are healings today.

Divine Healing Is Supported in Scripture

Even a casual reading of the four Gospels makes it evident that healing was the most prominent part of Jesus' earthly ministry. No physical infirmity, including blindness, and no disease, including leprosy, was considered beyond his power to heal. Even death itself was brought under his control, as in the case of Lazarus (John 11:1-44) and the son of the widow of Nain (Luke 7:11-17). Such power, of course, might be expected of God's own Son, but the New Testament clearly affirms that this privilege and blessing was extended to Jesus' disciples and to the Church for all time to come. It is helpful to examine some of the details of this teaching.

1. Not only did Jesus heal the sick but he also commissioned his disciples to "cure every kind of disease and sickness" (Matt. 10:1). The results of their ministry are reported in Mark 6:12-13: "They went out and preached that people should repent. They drove out many demons and anointed many sick people with oil and healed them." This healing ministry by Jesus' disciples continued after he had ascended into heaven. Acts 5:12-16 reports that "the apostles performed many miraculous signs and wonders among the people," and that "crowds gathered . . . bringing their sick . . . and all of them were healed." The time of miracles did not end with Jesus' ascension.

2. Healing is included among the "gifts" of the Holy Spirit. First Corinthians 12:4-11, 28-30 lists a number of such gifts. Healing is specifically mentioned in verses 9 and 30. Such gifts are not bestowed on persons for their own glory but are a manifestation of the power of the Holy Spirit. They are given for the common good of people and the upbuilding of the Church. The fact that some persons may be especially gifted in praying for the sick does not mean that divine healing can take place only through the prayers of such people. It is God who does the healing. Anyone who is a follower

of Christ can pray in faith. It is noteworthy that healing is mentioned in the same verse as the gift of faith—a gift to which every Christian can lay claim.

3. Healing, like salvation, is linked to the atoning death of Christ on the cross. Jesus himself suggests this relationship. In Matthew 8:16-17, he quotes and applies to himself the Isaiah 53:4 passage about the suffering servant who "took up our infirmities and carried our diseases." Then in Romans 8:23 Paul speaks of "the redemption of our bodies." The idea that divine physical healing is included in the Atonement raises some difficult questions. The most difficult would be the questions as to why some people are not healed, and why, ultimately, everyone is denied healing since all are appointed to die. These same questions would not apply to salvation since all who accept Christ will be saved and salvation is for eternity as well as this life. Obviously, the link between healing and the Atonement is not parallel with that of salvation, but it is still there. The Isaiah 53:4 and 1 Peter 2:24 passages, "by his wounds we are healed," give assurance that God's love and Christ's sacrifice include concern for physical as well as spiritual health.

4. Divine physical healing is an important aspect of the continuing ministry of the Church. The "gifts" of healing have been mentioned; these were to be exercised in the Church. In the Mark 16:18 version of the Great Commission Jesus is quoted as saying, "They will place their

hands on sick people, and they will get well."
(Even though some authorities question the
authenticity of this passage it is not out of
character with the "teaching them to obey everything I have commanded you" statement in
Matthew.) The strongest passage regarding the
continuing ministry of healing in the Church is,
of course, James 5:14-16. Here the practice is
not only advocated; it is ordered and the guidelines are spelled out—calling the elders—anointing with oil—the prayer of faith—the promise
that the Lord will raise up the afflicted person.

Practical Issues and Questions

The doctrine and practice of divine healing is
theologically sound and is clearly supported by
Scripture. It has been practiced in the Church
from New Testament times to the present but
there are still many questions about this subject
to which there may not be easy answers. It is
appropriate to note some of these and suggest
some possible answers.

1. If God is a God of love, always desiring
health and wholeness for his creation, why does
he allow or perhaps sometimes even send sickness to people who are living righteously and
striving to please their maker? The only answer
to this question is our assurance that, indeed,
God does will our ultimate good. His ways are
not always known to us. If we suffer affliction
for a time we can find comfort and strength in
the knowledge that he is working to achieve his
final purpose for us or others.

2. Why are some persons healed by prayers and others are not? This is perhaps the most persistent question in this area. In Jesus' ministry one can note in some of the cited passages the reference to "all" being healed; others refer only to specific persons. The disciples were not always successful (Matt. 17:19-20). Paul never received relief from his "thorn in the flesh" (whatever it was) and he left his friend Trophimus sick in Miletus (2 Tim. 4:20). James suggests possible reasons for failure to be healed as being lack of faith or asking for the wrong motives (James 4:3). Although these instances may be helpful (or comforting) they do not answer all the questions. (Note again the earlier discussion of healing in the Atonement.)

3. Can one expect healing for an illness resulting from neglect or abuse of the body? Any sickness that is brought on by knowing action can usually be cured by deliberate counteraction. If one is eating or drinking in a fashion harmful to the body, that can be changed. If one is working too hard or too long, schedule and habits can be altered. If one becomes ill because of worry or anxiety, he or she can learn to trust and relax. The same would be true regarding inadequate sleep, exercise, or diet. Right habits and self-discipline are important ingredients of good health. Even so, one can turn to God for healing—and then assume responsibility to see that illness does not come from these self-made causes again.

4. Is seeking medical aid a denial of faith in God for healing? It could be, but not necessarily.

God should not be put in the "last resort" position; he is just as available at the beginning of an illness as in its last stages. Even as one takes advantage of available human help in an illness there should be a strong sense of the presence of the Great Physician. One can also note that in our time God has enabled humankind to make great strides in combating many dread diseases; to fail to take advantage of available skills and knowledge might be considered deliberate personal neglect. It must be kept in mind, however, that nothing is too small or too large for God's concern and care. He is available for every need.

5. Is anointing with oil a necessary part of the procedure for divine healing? The admonition in James 5 is quite specific. However, many other New Testament accounts of healing and most of the promises in regard to healing do not mention anointing (Mark 11:44; John 15:7; John 16:23). In no reference is there any indication that the oil is curative. It is a symbol for one's faith. It would thus appear to be a desirable procedure but not a necessary one. In any case it is God who does the healing.

6. Who must exercise the faith for healing? Some insist that it must be the sick person's faith; others say it is the faith of the person who is praying. Most "professional" healers at least imply that it is their faith that brings the healing. The fact is that the Scriptures do not quibble on this point. The promise is based simply on "the prayer of faith," without reference to whose. A person who is in great pain or

even unconscious obviously would not be able to exercise faith, and so others would be required to do so. The answer: either the sick person or some other person, or both, must put their faith in God. The important thing is to pray believingly and expectantly.

7. Suppose one does all that is known to do and still is not healed—what then? There are many possible responses: bitterness, doubting or blaming God, asking "why me?" fatalistic resignation, refusal to admit the true situation, blaming one's self or others. This is the time to "hold on" to God, knowing that he still lives and loves. Recall Jesus' words in Gethsemane, "Not my will, but thine be done!"

Health and Wholeness

Although Jesus gave a great deal of attention to physical healing, the major focus of his ministry was on the whole person. Many of his healings were accompanied by forgiveness of sin— an obvious recognition of the close relationship between physical, spiritual, and mental health. So, long before the use of the psychological term, *psychosomatic,* Jesus was stressing the importance of the body-mind-spirit relationship. He came to bring health to all aspects of life.

A word needs to be said also about the concept of the human body as a "temple of God" (1 Cor. 6:19). This implies personal responsibility on the part of each person to treat his or her body with respect and even awe. The body is a wonderful and complex creation—a tribute to the intelligence of its maker. It deserves the best of treatment and care. It is interesting to note that early preachers in the Church of God movement usually carried three books as they traveled—a Bible, a songbook, and a health book. Along with preaching divine healing they instructed people regarding diet, exercise, and health habits. J. Grant Anderson's 1926 book *Divine Healing,* for instance, concluded with six laws of health: right eating, right drinking, right breathing, right thinking, right exercising, and right sleeping. This would not be a bad outline for a modern physical-fitness manual.

If, however, despite the best of care, the body should become the victim of injury, system failure, or disease, there is strong reassurance in the fact that "prayer offered in faith will make the sick person well; the Lord will raise him up."

Chapter 11

Eschatology (Last Things)

Biblical Resources

Matthew 4:17; 24:1-44; 25:31-46
Luke 1:32-33; 16:16; 17:20-21
John 5:28-29; 14:1-4; 18:36-37
Acts 1:9-11; 17:31; 24:14-16
Romans 2:11-16; 14:17-18
1 Corinthians 4:20; 15:35-58
Philippians 3:20-21
1 Thessalonians 4:13-16; 5:1-3
2 Thessalonians 1:7-10
Hebrews 9:27-28
1 Peter 4:7
2 Peter 1:11; 3:10
Revelation 1:7; 20:1-14; 22:7

For Study and Discussion

1. Why is it important for religious faith to

include some projection of what will take place in the future?

2. Define the word *apocalyptic*. Which books of the Bible include material that could be described as apocalyptic? Some apocryphal books (those not included in the canon) also contain such material. What bearing does this have on the interpretation of the biblical passages?

3. What is the meaning of Jesus' statement "The kingdom of God is within you?"

4. How should one respond to those who contend that the kingdom of God will not be established until the second coming of Christ?

5. Do the Scriptures provide a detailed sequence of events that will take place at the time Christ returns? Identify the main happenings.

6. Revelation 20 makes several references to a "thousand years." How is this to be interpreted?

7. On what basis will persons be judged at the end of time? Who will be judged?

8. Are the prospects of eternal reward or punishment an adequate basis for evangelism?

9. What is the full meaning of the term *the Christian hope?*

Suggested Group Activity

If the end of time were going to occur this Saturday at sunset, what would you do as an individual to prepare yourself? What would you do as a class or church?

Information and Issues

What is going to happen in the future? This is a question that has concerned every human being since time began. In its most basic and ultimate sense this is a religious question, for it relates to the meaning of life and death. It deals with final destiny. Consequently, Christianity, along with other religions, gives considerable attention to the future, both for individual persons and for the world.

In its concepts of the future, Christianity has been greatly influenced by views held in various segments of Judaism for several centuries prior and up to the time of Christ. The most dominant aspect of Jewish anticipation of the future was their expectation of a coming Messiah. All Jews were not in agreement, however, regarding what would happen when the Messiah arrived. One prominent view projected a time when the Jewish people would be freed from political oppression and be able to govern themselves, living in peace and prosperity. All their enemies would be either destroyed or controlled. In the thinking of some Jews the realization of this dream would bring in a "new age" and would include a "new earth." Even the forces of nature would join in contributing to the well-being and pleasure of the people. There would be no such things as drought or destructive storms. The fields and flocks would produce abundantly; physical comforts would be enjoyed by all. This new age would be ushered in after a great battle between the forces of good, led by the Messiah, and the forces of evil, led by Satan. The Messiah would be victorious, evil would be conquered, and righteousness would prevail for a thousand years. The reason why most Jews did not accept Jesus as the Messiah was that he, obviously, did not fit or fulfill these expectations.

This view of the future is known as *apocalypticism*—a word that means "revelation." Jewish writings that describe this kind of future age would include the Book of Daniel in the Old Testament, and the apocryphal Book of Enoch and Apocalypse of Baruch. Portions of other Old Testament books, such as Joel, Amos, and Zechariah, are also apocalyptic. (It is well to note that not all messianic writings are apocalyptic—only those that describe the new age in political and materialistic terms.) After the time of Christ there were several Christian writings, including some of the Gospel accounts of the teachings of Jesus, that followed the apocalyptic pattern. The chief of these, of course, is the New Testament Book of Revelation—the Apocalypse of John. Portions of the Gospels of Mark (chap. 13) and Matthew (chap. 24) are also apocalyptic. Other Christian writings of this type that were not included in the New Testament would be books like II Esdras, the Apocalypse of Paul, and the Shepherd of Hermas. These writings indicate that Jesus and many early Christians also had a vision of future cataclysmic events that would usher in a new age. Apocalypticism is thus at least a part of the Christian view of last things.

There is one feature that is common to all

apocalyptic literature—it utilizes symbols to convey intended meanings. The interpretation of these symbols would be known to the people for whom the document was written but would be no more than interesting fantasy to others, thus hiding the real meaning. This complicates the problem of interpretation by later readers who develop their own speculations about what the symbols mean. This factor has opened the door to the development of widely divergent views regarding Christian eschatology. Some Christian groups such as the Adventists, for example, base their whole reason for existence on particular views about what they think will take place in the future, and when these events are going to happen. The same, in a very unenlightened way, would be true of Jehovah's Witnesses. Other groups, such as dispensationalists and the various schools of millennial theory, have given major emphasis to interpreting the symbols and have built theological systems around their particular views. Some preachers, especially a few on radio and television, and some sensational writers make their own predictions about the return of Christ and the end of the world. Most of these seek to relate end-time events to newspaper headlines, with particular attention to happenings in the Middle East that relate to Israel and the Jewish people. Premillennialists, for example, seem to forget that the coming of Jesus ushered in the new covenant and base their whole dispensational system on the Abrahamic and Mosaic covenants that promised the eternal possession of the land of Canaan to Abraham and his descendants. Without a doubt there is no other Christian doctrine about which there is so much wild speculation and confusion.

It thus becomes very important to give careful attention to what the Bible actually teaches in regard to Christian eschatology. To avoid getting caught up in the fantasies of speculation, and to clarify what is often very confusing, one needs to examine the whole range of Christian teachings relating to the future. The whole picture of "last things" from a Christian biblical point of view has six basic ingredients. Each will be examined briefly.

The Kingdom of God

A proper understanding of Jesus' often-used term *the kingdom of God,* is basic to the whole issue of Christian eschatology. He mentioned the Kingdom frequently and used many parables to explain its meaning. The content of his teaching lifts up four major characteristics of the kingdom of God.

1. The Kingdom is spiritual and not political or geographical. It is the whole realm of God's rule in the universe. Luke 17:20-21 records Jesus' very explicit description of the Kingdom: "The kingdom of God does not come visibly, nor will people say, 'Here it is,' or 'There it is,' because the kingdom of God is within you." The Apostle Paul speaks in similar manner when he says, "The kingdom of God is not meat and drink; but righteousness, and peace, and joy in the Holy Ghost" (Rom. 14:17, KJV). Using a differ-

ent metaphor, he expresses the same thought: "The kingdom of God is not in word, but in power" (1 Cor. 4:20, KJV). Thus, unlike the church, which is visible, the kingdom of God is not visible to the natural eye. It exists wherever and in whomever the rule of God is known and received.

2. Christ is the initiator of the Kingdom in the sense the term is used in the New Testament. As the Messiah, he was the fulfillment of the Old Testament prophesies concerning the coming king. At the very beginning of his ministry Jesus announced, "The kingdom of heaven is at hand" (Matt. 4:17, KJV). The kingship of Christ was validated by his earthly ministry, his death, and his resurrection. He could rightfully claim the Kingdom, as in John 18:36-37 where he says, "My kingdom is not of this world. . . . You are right in saying I am a king. In fact, for this reason I was born, and for this I came into the world, to testify to the truth." This passage makes it clear that Christ indeed is king, but not of an earthly realm. "If it were," he said, "my servants would fight to prevent my arrest by the Jews." There certainly are no grounds for believing, as do some premillennialists, that earthly powers have any involvement in establishing God's kingdom. It already has been brought into being by Jesus Christ through the power of God.

3. The Kingdom is present—and has been so since the earthly ministry of Christ. Jesus declared, "The Law and the Prophets were proclaimed until John. Since that time, the good

news of the kingdom of God is being preached, and everyone is forcing his way into it" (Luke 16:16). Thus, the Old Testament prophecies were fulfilled in Christ and since his advent he has been reigning in the hearts of all redeemed persons. There is no need to wait for future events to take place in order for the Kingdom to be realized.

4. The kingdom of God is eternal. It is both present and future and is not limited by time or events. It cannot be confined to any future designated period—not even one of a thousand years. Second Peter 1:11 refers to God's "everlasting kingdom." In the words of the angel announcing Jesus' birth to Mary, "His kingdom will never end." It will not cease with the return of Christ and the end of time. It will continue through all eternity.

The Return of Christ

An important aspect of the faith of the early church was the anticipation that some time after Christ's ascension into heaven he would return again to earth. This expectation, with varying degrees of emphasis, has continued through all the centuries since that time. There are many scriptural passages that validate such anticipation. Before his crucifixion Jesus told his disciples, "And if I go and prepare a place for you, I will come back and take you to be with me that you also may be where I am" (John 14:3). The account of Jesus' ascension quotes the angel who proclaimed, "This same Jesus, who has been taken from you into heaven, will come back in the same way you have seen him go into heaven" (Acts 1:11). The Apostle Paul writes, "For the Lord himself will come down from heaven, with a loud command, with the voice of the archangel and with the trumpet call of God" (1 Thess. 4:16). In the Book of Revelation John writes, "Look, he is coming with the clouds, and every eye will see him" (1:7). There are many more references to the Second Coming.

With all this evidence there has not been much disagreement among Christians about the fact of Christ's return. There has been much disagreement, however, about the details of when, how many times, and what will happen after he arrives. There is really little need for speculation as to when this will happen. Jesus, after a rather long discourse on the "signs" of his coming and the end of the age (Matt. 24), plainly affirmed, "No one knows about that day or hour, not even the angels in heaven, nor the Son, but only the Father" (v. 36). Other texts speak of his coming as being unexpected, sudden, and "like a thief in the night" (1 Thess. 5:2). Even so, there has been much speculation and some prediction. It is clear that the early church expected this to happen quickly. At the close of his revelation John is told, twice, "Behold, I am coming soon!" (Rev. 22:7, 12). Through the centuries many people have set dates and made special preparations. Some contend that Christ has already returned. Others look forward to multiple returns, with intervals in between. Such speculations, whether by post-millennialists, premillennialists, or dispensation-alists have no basis in Scripture.

The End of Time

All of the scriptural references relating to Christ's return either state specifically or imply that his second coming will mark the end of this age of time. The question asked of Jesus by his disciples in Matthew 24:3 definitely links the two events together: "Tell us," they said, "when will this happen, and what will be the sign of your coming and of the end of the age?" First Peter 4:7 associates Christ's return with "the end of all things." A significant aspect of the end of this age, which apparently is overlooked by those anticipating another chance for repentance in a millennium, is the fact that the end of time will mark the termination of Christ's work of redemption. Hebrews 9:28 clearly affirms: "So Christ was sacrificed once to take away the sins of many people; and he will appear a second time, not to bear sin, but to bring salvation to those who are waiting for him." Thus, at Christ's second coming the age of grace and salvation will come to an end, along with the destruction of the world as we know it. The description in 2 Peter 3:10 reads, "The heavens will disappear with a roar; the elements will be destroyed by fire, and the earth and everything in it will be laid bare."

The Resurrection of the Dead

All the biblical accounts of what is projected

to happen on that "last day" include some reference to a resurrection of those who have died—an event in which the whole human race will be involved. None of the descriptions, however, provide a full agenda of events and their sequence. This has left room for scholars and others to try to piece together the sketchy accounts and add their own speculations about all that is likely to happen. In regard to the resurrection of the dead there are only two things that are clearly indicated in the scriptural accounts.

1. There will be a massive general resurrection of all human beings who have ever lived. Jesus is quoted in John 5:28-29 as saying, "Do not be amazed at this, for a time is coming when all who are in their graves will hear his voice and come out." The Apostle Paul affirms that "there will be a resurrection of both the righteous and the wicked" (Acts 24:15). The previously cited Revelation 1:7 adds emphasis by declaring, "Every eye will see him."

2. In the process of this general resurrection some of the sources indicate there will be a sequence. Paul states in regard to the coming of the Lord that "the dead in Christ will rise first" (1 Thess. 4:16). Jesus' words recorded in Matthew 24:30-31 speak of how his angels will "gather his elect from the four winds, from one end of the heavens to the other." Some interpreters have speculated that there will be a time lapse (some say seven years, others a thousand years) between the resurrection of the righteous and the resurrection of the wicked. No such

time lapse is clearly indicated in any of the Scriptures; Jesus' own words suggest an immediate sequence. After referring to "all who are in their graves" coming out, he says, "Those who have done good will rise to live, and those who have done evil will rise to be condemned" (John 5:29).

The Final Judgment

There is no teaching in the New Testament that is more fully attested than the fact of a last judgment. Underneath the whole message of the gospel is the basic assumption that every person is accountable to God for the deeds done in the body. Matthew 25:31-46 gives a very vivid account of the judgment scene—the separation of the "sheep" from the "goats" followed by a delineation between those on the right hand of the Son of man and those on his left. The basis of judgment is here defined as what has been done "to the least of these brothers of mine" (vv. 40, 45). Paul affirms that God "has set a day when he will judge the world with justice by the man he has appointed. He has given proof of this to all men by raising him from the dead" (Acts 17:31). The Revelation 20 account of the Judgment says, "Each person was judged according to what he had done" (v. 13).

The basic standard of judgment is the gospel. Jesus warned those who rejected him, "There is a judge for the one who rejects me and does not accept my words; that very word which I spoke will condemn him at the last day" (John 12:48). Paul reaffirms this by noting that "when the

Lord Jesus is revealed from heaven in blazing fire . . . he will punish those who do not know God and do not obey the gospel of our Lord Jesus" (2 Thess. 1:7-8).

There is very little guidance regarding the basis of judgment for those who have not heard the gospel. Paul touches on this issue in Romans 2:11-16. Speaking of the Gentiles, he makes note that "they show that the requirements of the law are written on their hearts, their consciences also bearing witness" (v. 15). This, he says, will be the basis of their judgment "on the day when God will judge men's secrets through Jesus Christ" (v. 16). In any case, for all persons the Judgment will be fair and just, based on reality and not appearances.

Reward and Punishment— Beyond Time to Eternity

The end of time is not the end of existence. Human identity and consciousness continue forever. The exact nature of the resurrected body is not known, but it will be different. Paul anticipated that Christ "will transform our lowly bodies so that they will be like his glorious body" (Phil. 3:21). This would imply an eternal body like that of the resurrected Lord—identifiable in form, yet spiritual and not subject to death. Paul further elaborates on this issue in 1 Corinthians 15, affirming that "the dead will be raised imperishable, and we will be changed. For the perishable must clothe itself with the imperishable, and the mortal with immortality" (vv. 52-53).

Continued existence, however, would be of little import without some reference to the character of that existence. It is at this point that the outcome of the final judgment becomes significant. Those judged to be righteous will be invited to participate in the joys of eternal life; those judged to be wicked will be condemned to eternal judgment and damnation. The reward of the righteous is designated as heaven; the punishment of the wicked is described as hell. Graphic word pictures of each of these are portrayed by several writers in both the Old and New Testaments. Some of these pictures are quite sensual and materialistic, such as "streets of gold, walls of jasper and gates of pearl" for heaven and "the lake that burneth with fire and brimstone" for hell. How much of this language is symbolic and how much is literal, we do not really know. We can be assured, however, that heaven will be good, for we will be with the Lord. We can be equally sure that hell will be bad, for we will be separated from Christ forever.

Our faith in the future, as Christians, is not based on a Kodacolor picture of the hereafter; it is based on the promise of the gospel. We know that "Jesus saves"—for time and eternity. We know that accepting or rejecting Christ as Savior is each person's decision. We also know that we shall be ultimately judged "according to the deeds done in the body." We can count on the fact that eternity is forever. Consequently, we can say along with the Apostle Paul, "So I strive always to keep my conscience clear before God and man" (Acts 24:16).

No one on earth really knows the future, but we do know that there will be a future for every person—either in this life or in eternity. With this in mind it is well to ponder Paul's appropriate conclusion to his beautiful discourse on the future: "Therefore, my dear brothers, stand firm. Let nothing move you. Always give yourselves fully to the work of the Lord, because you know that your labor in the Lord is not in vain" (1 Cor. 15:58).

Chapter 12

Christian Discipleship
and Mission

Biblical Resources

Matthew 11:28-29; 25:14-46; 28:19
Mark 10:17-22
Luke 9:2; 10:1-20; 14:26-27, 33
John 3:16; 10:10; 13:34-35
Acts 1:8
Romans 10:12-15
2 Corinthians 8:5
2 Timothy 4:5
1 John 3:16-18

For Study and Discussion

1. Explain what is meant by a "Christian doctrine of deeds and action."

2. Define the full meaning of the word *disciple* as Jesus used it.

3. What did Jesus really mean when he said that his disciples should "hate" members of their own family?

4. What is the relationship between stewardship and discipleship?

5. Jesus told his disciples, "Love one another." What and who is included in one's expression of this love?

6. What is the difference between being a disciple and being a "missioner?" What is the difference between "the Christian mission" and "Christian missions?"

7. Can one be a missionary without going to a foreign land? Explain your answer.

8. What are some of the most significant ways one can effectively witness to faith in Jesus Christ?

9. Paul admonished Timothy to "do the work of an evangelist" (2 Tim. 4:5). What is the work of an evangelist?

10. What is the difference between serving the needs of others in the name of Christ and doing good deeds to earn "merit" for salvation?

Suggested Group Activity

Select at ramdom articles from a newspaper that describe needy situations. Discuss what the situation really needs—from the point of view that you are Jesus' disciples. Is there some action that you could take?

Information and Issues

In speaking of "doctrine" one usually thinks of that which relates only to the mind—precepts that have been set forth as being true—tenets of faith—things believed. In the strictest sense this limited meaning is proper. The word *doctrine* literally means a "teaching" or a "theory." In a more complete sense, however, doctrine relates to every part of one's person—to the mind, of course, but also to the will, to feelings, to commitments, to actions. It involves heart and hands and feet as well as head. It concerns what one does, where one goes, how one acts. Unless what one thinks motivates action in accordance with beliefs and convictions, then head doctrine means very little, regardless of how "right" those beliefs might be. So it is perfectly proper to speak of a Christian doctrine of deeds and action. In this context it is well to remember that Jesus, along with being a teacher, was a man of action. He taught the basic theological understandings about God, salvation, the Church, the Kingdom, and the future; he then demonstrated the meaning of these as he related to people, served their needs, and gave his own life for the salvation of others. Out of this blending of theology with behavior there emerges a basis for a Christian perspective on ethics, morals, lifestyle, interpersonal relations, social responsibility, outreach, and witness. It is at these points that the Christian faith becomes most visible, moving from precept to practice, from views to virtues, from academics to action.

There has not been a consistently strong emphasis regarding this aspect of the Christian faith either in Christian history or among various contemporary groups. In modern times the degree of attention to societal issues has been a matter of considerable debate, and even division, among Christians. Some have focused primarily on action and have been labeled as proponents of a "social gospel." Others have elevated an emphasis on personal salvation to the point of ignoring any Christian responsibility for dealing with the problems of society. In regard to this debate the Church of God, throughout its history, has sought to avoid the extremes of an "either/or" position and to maintain some degree of a "both/and" stance. As an evangelical movement there, of course, has been great and often major attention to personal salvation. At the same time, as proponents of holy living, the aspect of Christian service has not been neglected. Considerable concern has been shown in ministering to the needs of hurting humanity and striving to right the wrongs of injustice and discrimination in society. Other evangelical and holiness groups have been roused to a social consciousness only in very recent years, while the Church of God has carried something of this concern from its beginning. Thus, it is with good reason that this be included as one of the distinguishing doctrines of the movement.

Even a very casual analysis of this topic makes it obvious that there are many facets to a Christian doctrine of deeds. Further thought, however, reveals that all of the important aspects can be brought together adequately in just two words: *discipleship* and *mission.* These words are closely interrelated, yet there is a sufficient difference of meaning between them to warrant defining and elaborating on each of them separately.

Discipleship

A disciple is a follower; a disciple is a learner. To be a disciple of Christ, then, is to be a follower of Jesus and a learner from Jesus. The essence of Christian discipleship is that one becomes an eager student of Christ the master teacher, reflects his spirit, is captivated by his ideal, and is led to act in accordance with his teachings. Jesus issued an open invitation to discipleship. "Come to me," he said. "Take my yoke upon you and learn from me, for I am gentle and humble in heart" (Matt. 11:28-29). Discipleship thus means responding to Jesus' call, taking on his yoke (work), and learning from him. In the calling of his own disciples—the "twelve" and many others—and in his public teaching Jesus had a great deal to say about discipleship. In many ways he made it plain that following him was not easy; he held out no lures of comfortable living or earthly gain. In fact, on several occasions he made a special point of emphasizing how hard it is to be one of his disciples. At least five things stand out in Jesus' teachings regarding the meaning of discipleship.

1. One must make a realistic assessment of the cost of being a disciple. One of the best examples of this requirement is Jesus' reply to

the rich young ruler (Mark 10:17 ff). It is obvious that the young man was greatly attracted by the things he heard Jesus say. He was a serious seeker. He really wanted to be a disciple but he was not prepared to pay the price. When he learned the cost, the account says, "the man's face fell. He went away sad" (v. 22). Jesus wants no unthinking or shallow decisions. The point is again made clear in the illustration about a man who wants to build a tower. "Will he not," asks Jesus, "first sit down and estimate the cost to see if he has enough money to complete it?" (Luke 14:28). Discipleship is more than a decision to try following Christ; it is a commitment to go with him all the way—even to the end of one's life.

2. One must make following Christ the item of highest priority in his or her whole life. Jesus' teaching on this point is very specific and, when one first reads it, may sound unreasonably harsh. For instance, on one occasion Jesus turned to the large crowds following him and said, "If anyone comes to me and does not hate his father and mother, his wife and children, his brothers and sisters—yes, even his own life—he cannot be my disciple" (Luke 14:26). Biblical scholars refer to this as one of the "hard sayings" of Jesus. If the word *hate* is interpreted literally it is a very hard statement. It is quite clear, however, that Jesus' intent was to give strong emphasis to the truth that discipleship must be the highest priority item in one's life. One's relationship to God is more important than any other. He confirms this

intention a few sentences later when he says, "Any of you who does not give up everything he has cannot be my disciple" (v. 33). The "let the dead bury their own dead" teaching of Matthew 8:18-22 and Luke 9:57-62 conveys the same message.

3. One must accept and perform the specific divine tasks and responsibilities to which God calls. This may not be easy; for Jesus the task was giving his own life. He used this as a symbol of the tasks to which his disciples are called. "If anyone would come after me," he said, "he must deny himself and take up his cross and follow me" (Matt. 16:24). On another occasion he told his followers, "And anyone who does not carry his cross and follow me cannot be my disciple" (Luke 14:27). For some the calling may be to a full-time religious vocation—preacher, teacher, missionary. For all, Christian discipleship means the translation of all one's theological understandings into attitudes and actions. It means living one's beliefs—in both thought and deed. It means following Christ every hour of every day in every circumstance, with no lapses or deviations. A true disciple follows Christ in every aspect of his or her life-style—work, leisure, friendships, interests. It involves the deliberate cultivation of close relationships with God through frequent prayer, Bible study, and meditation. Discipleship thus means a commitment to carry out one's God-given responsibilities—even unto death.

4. One must become a person who lives and acts as a good steward of all his or her resources. This includes one's own body and mind, health, strength, skills, time, and possessions. Unless one's faith functions in temporal and material terms it does not really function. A good steward is concerned about the production, conservation, and proper use of all resources at his or her disposal. Here again, Jesus gives some very specific guidance, this time in the form of a parable. In the story of the talents (Matt. 25:14-30) he makes it plain that, even though every person may not have the same resources, each one is responsible for the profitable use of what he or she has. Good stewardship includes sharing with those in need and giving for the furtherance of God's work in the world. The Apostle Paul put it well when he spoke of the people in the churches of Macedonia: "They gave as much as they were able, and even beyond their ability. . . . And they did not do so as we expected, but they gave themselves first to the Lord and then to us in keeping with God's will" (2 Cor. 8:3, 5). Discipleship means the recognition that everything belongs to God and we are responsible for using all that is in our control for his glory.

5. One must accept, with all its implications, the basic premise that discipleship demands a loving involvement with others. Love is the central theme of all of Jesus' teaching. He put it very plainly when he said, "A new commandment I give you: Love one another. As I have loved you, so you must love one another. All

men will know that you are my disciples if you love one another" (John 13:34-35). Loving, then, is the real test—the tangible evidence that one is a disciple of Christ. This means loving across all the barriers that separate people from one another—race, class, color, status, language, or nationality. Without love between people, tribes, and nations, peace can never be achieved. Love is the only lasting basis for real brotherhood and fellowship. This expansive outreaching love is the basic motivation for all Christian service; it is the driving force for the Christian mission into all the world.

Mission

The word *mission* means "to send" or "to be sent" on some special assignment or for some designated task. In a Christian sense mission means being sent forth to share the gospel of Christ, to invite others to accept Christ as Savior and Lord, to minister to needy persons in the name of Christ, and to oppose evil in all its forms. In speaking of "the Christian mission" it is important to note that this term is much broader in scope and deeper in meaning than the commonly used reference to "Christian missions." The latter is used in a more limited sense to describe the organized efforts of various groups to "propagate the gospel" throughout the world. The persons who are sent—usually by churches or societies to other lands to evangelize and serve are properly called missionaries. They go at the request of some sending church or agency. "The Christian mission," however, is not confined to the work of these organized programs; it applies to every Christian. Each person who becomes a disciple of Christ is sent forth into the world to be a witness to his or her faith. This includes publicly living the way of Christ in all ways, evangelizing those who are "lost" because they do not know of Christ or have not accepted him as Savior and Lord, and serving human needs in the name of Christ.

Since every committed Christian is "sent" to carry out these assignments it would be appropriate, then, to refer to all who profess a saving knowledge of Christ as "missioners," leaving the designation of "missionary" to apply only to that limited number of persons who are sent by some mission agency. Such a delineation would immediately raise the question, of course, "Who sends the missioner?" Fortunately, at this point there is a considerable amount of good guidance in the New Testament. To begin with, it is well to note that Jesus himself was a sender. He called the Twelve to follow him and he also "sent them out to preach the kingdom of God and to heal" (Luke 9:2). After receiving his instructions, it is reported that "they departed and went through the villages, preaching the gospel and healing everywhere" (v. 6, RSV). In addition, he enlisted many more followers—seventy-two of them—and sent them out, two by two, on a similar mission (Luke 10:1-20). They also went forth and "returned with joy, saying, 'Lord, even the demons are subject to us in your name!' " (v. 17, RSV).

The region to which these followers of Jesus were sent was limited to Palestine, but the geographic area was widened considerably in the final commands of Jesus. Following the Resurrection he appeared to his disciples in Galilee and instructed them: "Go therefore and make disciples of all nations" (Matt. 28:19, RSV). Then, just before his ascension he reaffirmed the responsibility of those who would follow him. "You shall receive power when the Holy Spirit has come upon you; and you shall be my witnesses in Jerusalem and in all Judea and Samaria and to the end of the earth" (Acts 1:8). This leaves no room for doubt regarding who the "sender" is or the scope of where those being sent are to go. The missioner goes out under the authority of Christ and witnesses in his name.

The dynamic force behind the command to "go" is also made very clear. It is best expressed in the New Testament's most-often-repeated verse, John 3:16 (note the italicized words): "For God so *loved* the *world* that he gave his only Son, that *whoever* believes in him should not perish but have eternal life" (RSV). The expected response to this kind of love is indicated in 1 John 3:16: "By this we know love, that he laid down his life for us; and we ought to lay down our lives for the brethren" (RSV). The global target of this mission and its potential impact is well described by the Apostle Paul: "For there is no distinction between Jew and Greek; the same Lord is Lord of all and bestows his riches upon all who call upon him. For, 'every one who calls upon the name of the Lord will be saved' " (Rom. 10:12-13, RSV). What a challenge for the missioner!

From these biblical references, and other passages with a similar message, it becomes apparent that there are three interrelated aspects of the Christian mission: witness, evangelization, and service. All of these have the same purpose—to make Christ known to all persons on the earth so that they may believe in him and have eternal life. In a sense, these are but three different methods for achieving this same goal. A brief look at the specific meaning of each of these can help clarify how they relate to each other and how they implement the Christian mission.

1. Witness. A witness is one who gives testimony in regard to what he or she knows. When Jesus said, "You shall be my witnesses," he was saying that those who follow him are obligated to tell other people what they know about him. Those who have been redeemed have good news to share. Those who have experienced salvation want to and must tell others how it happened. The "telling" is done in many ways: verbally, of course, but also by actions, attitudes, and quality of life. There really is no such thing as a "secret" Christian. All of the qualities of discipleship that have been mentioned serve the double purpose of spiritual enhancement for the individual missioner as well as a public testimony to what Christ can do in the life of one of his followers. Even a person whose range

of public contact is quite limited can enlarge his witness by helping to send other witnesses—literature (especially Bibles), missionaries, and organized service programs.

2. Evangelization. The word *disciple* is usually used as a noun; it can also be a verb. To "disciple" others means to lead them in becoming a follower of Christ also. In the fullest sense the meaning of evangelization includes not only the proclamation of the gospel, but also teaching in regard to the meaning of accepting Christ and demonstrating a disciplelike life-style. It involves both this winning of individuals and the planting of congregations—congregations that, in turn become centers for winning new converts, nurturing them in Christian growth, and then sending them out as more witnesses (missioners) to start the whole procedure over again. Paul describes the evangelization cycle in this way: "How, then, can they call on the one they have not believed in? And how can they believe in the one of whom they have not heard? And how can they hear without someone preaching to them? And how can they preach unless they are sent? As it is written, 'How beautiful are the feet of those who bring good news!' " (Rom. 10:14-15). Every Christian is both disciple and discipler, both sent and sender. All are called by God to be evangelists, sharing the gospel with those who have not yet experienced the saving grace of Jesus Christ.

3. Service. It is Christ's intention that every person should have a meaningful and fulfilling life. Jesus said, "I came that they may have life,

and have it abundantly" (John 10:10, RSV). Unfortunately, the various social and economic systems of the world do not provide an opportunity for "abundant" life for all people. In every nation of the world, both developed and developing, there are millions of poor people. There are the diseased and crippled, the victims of discrimination and injustice, those exploited by the greed and dishonesty of those in power, and the great hordes who are hungry, ill-clothed, and ill-housed. To these deprived people, and to millions of others who are lonely, disturbed, and beset by personal and family problems, the Christian has a double ministry— to tell them about Christ as Savior, and to minister to their needs in his name. The Apostle John records Jesus' words, "If anyone has material possessions and sees his brother in need but has no pity on him, how can the love of God be in him? Dear children, let us not love with words or tongue but with actions and in truth" (1 John 3:17-18).

The most crucial point regarding Christian service to those in need is that it is a factor in destiny. In his last discourse to his disciples Jesus describes the separation of the righteous from the wicked at the time of the final judgment (Matt. 25:31-46). He identifies the righteous as those who have ministered to "the least of these brothers of mine" by feeding the hungry, giving drink to the thirsty, welcoming the stranger, clothing the naked, caring for the sick, and visiting those in prison. These are the ones who will inherit "the kingdom prepared for you since the creation of the world" (v. 34). Those who have failed to do these things "will go away to eternal punishment" (v. 46). For anyone, then, who wants to be a disciple of Christ through eternity, loving service to others is not an option; it is an integral part of the Christian mission.

Thus the Christian faith is not just a set of beliefs to be accepted; it is a Person to be followed and a mission to be accomplished.

Chapter 13

A Growing Faith

Biblical Resources

John 8:32; 14:16-17; 16:13-15
1 Corinthians 13:11
Ephesians 4:13-16
Philippians 2:12-13; 3:12-16; 4:8
2 Thessalonians 1:3-4
2 Timothy 2:15; 4:1-5
Hebrews 5:14
1 Peter 2:2-3; 3:15
2 Peter 1:5-9; 3:17-18
1 John 2:14; 5:6

For Study and Discussion

1. What specific responsibilities regarding one's religious beliefs are placed on a person who is not asked to subscribe to a prepared or prescribed statement of faith?

2. Evaluate the statement "When growth stops, death begins." In what ways would this principle apply to spiritual growth?

3. Everyone recognizes that times and circumstances change. Does truth change? Defend your answer.

4. What are the modern implications of Paul's admonition to Timothy: "Do your best to present yourself . . . as . . . a workerman . . . who correctly handles the word of truth" (2 Tim. 2:15)?

5. How does one deal with the many conflicting opinions about the meaning of almost every area of biblical "truth?" Should one avoid any contact with views other than those one already holds?

6. How can one be sure that he or she is being guided by the Holy Spirit in matters of faith and belief?

7. Often one hears the remark, "Experience is the best teacher." Evaluate this statement as it relates to one's religious beliefs.

8. What do you think Jesus meant when he said, "The truth will set you free?" In what ways is truth liberating today?

9. At what age could one say that spiritual maturity has been fully attained?

Suggested Group Activity

What are you doing to continue your spiritual growth? Are there things you are doing besides attending this Bible study? Share ideas of what might be done. When? How long? Where?

Information and Issues

From its beginning the Church of God reformation movement has affirmed a basic commitment, not just to certain "truths," but to all truth contained in the Word of God. This comprehensive and idealistic objective was specifically articulated in Daniel S. Warner's 1878 declaration that he felt the Lord had given him "a new commission to join holiness and all truth together" for the purpose of building up "the apostolic church of the living God." This declared aspiration to know and practice "all truth" set the tone for all the rest of the movement's history. There are several implications and by-products of such a stance.

In the first place, it fosters a climate of openness. It presumes that there is more truth yet to be discovered and apprehended. Consequently, there is an expectation that one can and should grow in understanding and applying all aspects of spiritual truth. Second, it makes the Christian church a community of serious seekers for truth. Rather than having the "official" content of Christian belief given in the form of an approved creed, a person is pointed to the whole of Scripture and told that this is "the mine from which you are to dig" for spiritual truth. Thus, the responsibility is placed on every Christian to seek and discover those truths that relate to life and salvation. The Apostle Paul admonished the Christians at Philippi to "continue to work out your salvation with fear and trembling" (Phil. 2:12). Even that which is true has little meaning for a person until that person has made it his or her own. Truth must be learned, of course, but it also must be personalized and woven into the fabric of one's own experience.

Another implication of this commitment to all truth is that it leaves room for a degree of tentativeness about some beliefs—particularly those that are interpreted in a wide variety of ways by different groups of Christians. In the midst of this great array of diverse opinions it is sometimes difficult to arrive at what is felt to be solid ground. Some persons find this to be an uncomfortable position since they would rather have someone tell them what they should believe. This reliance on outside authority may be a good way to handle some issues, at least temporarily. For the basic convictions that guide one's life and destiny there is no substitute for a self-developed theology. This is not the easiest way. It is the best way whether one feels comfortable or not in doing it. To provide some help in this life-long personal quest for truth, the following seven guidelines for living in the continuous tension of Christian growth are offered.

1. Accept the Necessity for Spiritual Growth

Persons who have been taught in the "holiness" tradition have sometimes neglected to give adequate attention to the need for Christian growth in the area of belief. There has been a strong emphasis on the biblical teachings regarding experiential sanctification and Christian perfection. This has tended to overshadow the equally important need for continuous attention to "going on" in matters of belief and behavior. This, too, is solidly biblical.

Among the New Testament writers the Apostle Peter looms large as a strong advocate of spiritual growth. Perhaps this is because he himself was faced with the necessity of "growing" by altering some of his deeply held earlier convictions. The issue of including Gentiles in the fellowship of Christians is a good example (Acts 10 and 15). Consequently, in his letters Peter is quite specific regarding the necessity for Christian growth. To the churches throughout Asia Minor he wrote, "Like newborn babies, crave pure spiritual milk, so that by it you may grow up in your salvation, now that you have tasted that the Lord is good" (1 Pet. 2:2-3). In his second letter, addressed to all Christians, he closes with a warning against "the error of lawless men" and then strongly urges, "But grow in the grace and knowledge of our Lord and Savior Jesus Christ" (2 Pet. 3:18).

Earlier Peter had indicated one of the primary purposes behind this diligent concern for becoming grounded in the faith and alert to all the new attacks that were being directed toward these young churches. That purpose relates not only to one's own stability but also to evangelistic witness. "Always be prepared," he admonishes, "to give an answer to everyone who asks you to give the reason for the hope that you have" (1 Pet. 3:15). To be able to do this requires a well-developed personal faith that has been updated so as to withstand the arguments of all who would distort the gospel or seek to discredit Christ. Growth in both grace and knowledge is a necessity.

2. Focus Central Attention on Christ

Any plan of spiritual growth requires the identification of certain goals and objectives. For the Christian there is really only one option in this regard. The writer of Ephesians states it well when he says that the goal will not be attained "until we all reach unity in the faith and in the knowledge of the Son of God and become mature, attaining to the whole measure of the fullness of Christ" (Eph. 4:13). He goes further to describe the scope of this goal by saying, "We will in all things grow up into him who is the Head, that is, Christ" (v. 15). What a model to imitate!

Such a growth goal may, at first, seem unrealistic. When one looks at such phrases as "attaining to the full measure of the fullness of Christ" and "in all things grow up into him who is the Head," it would appear that this would be projecting an impossible ideal. But one must remember that Jesus was a man as well as God. Jesus must be seen in his long and deep struggle with temptation, in his agony in Gethsemane, and in his painful cry of forsakenness on the cross. He had to make difficult choices. He knew the pain of rejection even by his closest friends. It was by demonstrating his responsible maturity as a man that he was able to fulfill his divine purpose. Every Christian stands at this same point—faced with the challenge of fulfilling God's will for his or her own life.

The implications of focusing on Christ as an ideal are many. It keeps one's attention on what is really important. Many people are attracted by passing theological fads, single-issue religion, interesting incidentals, and even cults. The Ephesian writer describes persons who allow this to happen to them as "infants, tossed back and forth by the waves, and blown here and there by every wind of teaching and by the cunning and craftiness of men in their deceitful scheming" (Eph. 4:14). Focusing on Christ keeps one on the "main track" and insures stability. Then, too, Christlikeness is winsome and contagious, enabling one to be a living witness to what God's love can do in a person's life. With Christ as the center, the other important aspects of one's living and thinking can take their proper place at lower levels of priority. In the strictest sense it is only by taking Christ as the model for all aspects of one's life that he or she can be called Christian. Jesus must be at the center. Emulating Christ is not an impossible ideal, but it does leave plenty of room for growth.

3. Search for Sustenance

Growth of any kind is not automatic; it does not happen without some kind of intentional input and the providing of a suitable environment. Physical growth obviously requires adequate and proper food and water, as well as protection from extreme temperatures and other enemies of survival. Spiritual growth, likewise, requires nourishment and encouragement. The nourishment comes primarily from the study and application of Scripture; the encouragement comes primarily from the Church, other Christians—the strong encouraging the weak, the mature in faith helping new believers. At this point it is well to note also that spiritual nourishment must be appropriate for the person receiving it. The writer of Hebrews, after chastising his readers for their failure to grow spiritually, tells them they are still at the level of living on "milk" rather than the "solid food" they ought to be taking. "Anyone who lives on milk," he says, "being still an infant, is not acquainted with the teaching about righteousness. But solid food is for the mature, who by constant use have trained themselves to distinguish good from evil" (Heb. 5:13-14). Thus, the more one matures, the "meatier" should be this spiritual nourishment.

Paul's letters to the young Timothy include several examples of encouragement to spiritual growth. In the first place he identifies his relationship to Timothy: "You then, my son," he says, "be strong in the grace that is in Christ Jesus. And the things you have heard me say in the presence of many witnesses entrust to reliable men who will also be qualified to teach others" (2 Tim. 2:1-2). It should be noted that Timothy also is to teach "reliable men" so that they, in turn, may teach others. Thus, every Christian has the need to be fed spiritually as well as to share that food with others.

Paul then goes on to counsel Timothy more specifically in regard to growth. "Do your best," he says, "to present yourself to God as one approved, a workman who does not need to be ashamed and who correctly handles the word of truth" (v. 15). He thus highlights again the central truth that the primary source for spiritual growth is the word of God. He also emphasizes the fact that the prepared workman is one who "correctly handles the word of truth." This preparation requires study of the Word. Such study may be through formal schooling—college, seminary, or graduate studies. It may be training under a capable tutor, as was the case with Timothy. It may be diligent study on one's own with the aid of scholarly books and commentaries. In any case, Christian growth requires this basic spiritual food—the Word of God. After study, Paul then tells Timothy to "preach the Word; be prepared in season and out of season" (4:2).

Another source of nourishment for growth is also suggested to Timothy. Paul tells him, "Reflect on what I am saying, for the Lord will give you insight into all this" (2:7). Prayerful meditation is a means by which the Holy Spirit may guide one to deeper understandings. In addition to scholarly study, then, it can be very spiritually nourishing to reflect on what one hears and reads so that meanings are enhanced and applications of the Word are expanded.

4. Interact with the Best Minds of the Ages

Keeping the study of Scripture as basic, one can also turn to other valuable sources for instruction, enlargement of vision, edification, and inspiration. In the quest for truth there is no need to start at the beginning. Most of today's problems have been faced before, and some of them have been solved. There is no need to do battle with enemies that have already been conquered and it is folly to repeat the mistakes of past generations. The wise person will explore the vast field of human experience and aspiration, and use it as nourishment for his or her own growth.

To take full advantage of this wealth of accumulated wisdom one must study the history of the world's people and cultures, of one's own nation and other nations, and particularly the history of Christianity. It is important to know and appreciate those who have kept the torch of truth burning through these twenty centuries. Ireneus, Athanasius, Augustine, Thomas à Kempis, Luther, Calvin, Fox, Wesley, Warner, Byrum, Tillich, and many others should be more than names on a page; they need to be met through their writings, reacted to, and evaluated. By engaging in dialogue with the best thinkers of ages past, one's own thinking can be tested, deepened, and strengthened.

The Apostle Paul gives some valuable guidance for checking the validity of one's own opinions and evaluating the things one reads and hears. In writing to the Philippians he sets forth the following criteria: "Whatever is true, whatever is noble, whatever is right, whatever is pure, whatever is lovely, whatever is admirable—if anything is excellent or praiseworthy—think about such things" (4:8). If these qualifications are met, then that which is heard or read can be used for intellectual and spiritual profit; that which does not pass the test can be rejected. It is well to note further, however, that one can learn from those who express opinions quite different from one's own. Paul, for instance, wanted everyone to agree with the things he wrote but he realized that not everyone would. To these he wrote, "And if on some point you think differently, that too God will make clear to you" (Phil. 3:15).

5. Keep Open to the Leadings of the Holy Spirit

The key concept underlying the expectation of a growing faith is that the Holy Spirit indeed continues to guide persons into all truth. To accept the promise of Jesus (John 16:13) is to expect that God, through the Holy Spirit, will keep the channels of revelation open for those who seek him. It must not be presumed that God, in a sense, dumped the whole of divine truth on his creation during a certain period in history. Although truth itself does not change, God continues to intervene and respond. Consider God's response in the Old Testament to changing conditions, situations, and problems that the free-will decisions of humankind have created. This means that along with past revelations of truth in Scripture and history there is, through the Holy Spirit, a contemporary point of reference.

The Apostle John speaks of the Holy Spirit not only as the conveyer of truth but also as truth itself. He declares, "It is the Spirit who testifies, because the Spirit is the truth" (1 John 5:6). This identification of the Holy Spirit with truth is both awesome and exciting, for, as noted earlier, the Spirit is not only with us but can come to dwell in us. This makes the Counselor constantly available. It makes one's theology experiential. It means that God is still at work in human affairs and in the lives of his people. It means that one can seek and find guidance in applying one's faith to every circumstance, issue, and problem. It means that, if one is open to such guidance, continuing revelation of God's truth is available.

The capstone of this divine-human relationship is gloriously affirmed in the promise of Jesus to his disciples. "I will ask the Father," he said, "and he will give you another Counselor to be with you forever—the Spirit of truth" (John 14:16-17). "Forever" includes the present and the future for all time.

6. Build on Experience

There are certain natural sequences in growth. The elementary must be mastered before moving to the more advanced. One must go through states of progression—from child to adult, from beginner to skilled practitioner, from new convert to mature Christian. Upward movement from one stage to another is aided by all the things mentioned earlier, but the most convincing element in growth is the practical ingredient—one's own experience. Successes and failures in trying something new contribute greatly to one's progress toward maturity. This is as true in spiritual growth as it is in any other kind of growth.

The already mentioned reference in Hebrews of moving beyond "milk" to "solid food" (5:12-14) is an illustration of the need for this kind of spiritual progression. Solid food is for the mature and the milk is no longer needed. The Apostle Paul, likewise, notes the progress of his own growth by experience. "When I was a child," he says, "I talked like a child, I thought like a child, I reasoned like a child. When I became a man, I put childish ways behind me" (1 Cor. 13:11). Thus growth involves leaving behind certain earlier understandings and moving on to more mature concepts. Often the criterion for what is left and what is added is experience.

The Apostle Peter provides a formula for deliberate progression from one aspect of spiritual experience to another: "Add to your faith goodness; and to goodness, knowledge; and to knowledge, self-control; and to self-control, perseverance; and to perseverance, godliness; and to godliness, brotherly kindness; and to brotherly kindness, love. For if you possess these qualities in increasing measure, they will keep you from being ineffective and unproductive in your knowledge of our Lord Jesus Christ" (2 Pet. 2:5-8). Paul adds to this experiential formula by saying, "Let us live up to what we have already attained" (Phil. 3:16).

7. Expect Progress

A growing faith is always accompanied by an attitude of expectation. Every day holds the prospect of something new—new insights, new opportunities, new applications of the gospel, new decisions, new ways to witness and serve. When one begins to feel, as the Apostle John puts it, that "the word of God lives in you" (1 John 2:14), there is a sense of anticipation and adventure. One's theology begins to excite as well as inform; it inspires as well as instructs; it stirs the heart as well as stimulates the mind. In spite of the awareness that there may be changes tomorrow, there is not a feeling of uncertainty or tentativeness. The place where one stands is solid and firm, but the challenge to step up to a higher platform may come at any time.

A growing faith is accompanied by growth in other areas of the Christian life. Paul commends the people in the Thessalonian church. He says, "Your faith is growing more and more, and the love every one of you has for each other is increasing" (2 Thess. 1:3). The "growing faith—growing love" formula is exciting. It moves one beyond sympathetic concern to caring action. It moves beyond theology as a set of propositions that must be defended to a faith to be lived and shared. It moves beyond beliefs that are held to convictions that motivate to action.

The excitement of a growing faith is heightened by a sense of freedom. Jesus invited the Jews of his day to accept his teachings and become his disciples. "Then," he promised, "you will know the truth, and the truth will set you free" (John 8:32). He was telling them that the Christian faith is liberating—it not only frees one from the guilt of past sins, but also gives freedom from the binding forces of tradition, human opinions, and legalisms. In Christ one is free to grow and should expect to grow.

A Life-long Journey and Quest

Christian theology is an academic course in which one enrolls but always carries an "incomplete." It is a journey and not a destination. One can never say, "I have arrived!" Even the Apostle Paul, near the end of his life, was impelled to say, "I press on to take hold of that for which Christ Jesus took hold of me. Brothers, I do not consider myself yet to have taken hold of it" (Phil. 3:12-13). For him as well as for us, Christian faith is a continuing quest and not just a single discovery. While holding fast to what we know we never give up the search for more of God's truth. We continue to seek for a more complete understanding of his Word, and for a fuller knowledge of what he wants us to do. We can then join Paul in declaring, "I press on toward the goal for the prize of the upward call of God in Christ Jesus" (v. 14, RSV). A growing theology is one that keeps us "pressing on"—responding to the upward call of God.

The result of this "onward and upward" quest may not be a neat and polished systematic theology, but it will be a faith—a faith that excites, a faith that sings, a faith that comforts, a faith that means as much on Monday as it does on Sunday, a faith so strong that it will never break. Yet, it is flexible enough to include a brother or sister whose views are different. It is a faith that glows in the heart and sends messages to the hands and feet—and purse—to go forth and do the work of the Lord.

Such an exhilarating experience can never be realized, however, if one continues to think in terms of "the faith." It must become personal—"my faith!" It is my faith that I am working out "with fear and trembling." Then I can know that God is at work in me, "both to will and work for his good pleasure" (Phil. 2:12-13, paraphrased).